SMALL ARMS

OF WORLD WAR II

SMALL ARMS
OF WORLD WAR II

Chris Chant

Grange BOOKS

This edition published in 2001 by Grange Books
Grange Books plc
The Grange
1–6 Kingsnorth Estate
Hoo
Near Rochester
Kent ME3 9ND

www.grangebooks.co.uk

ISBN 1-84013-443-7

Editorial and design:
Brown Partworks Limited
8 Chapel Place
Rivington Street
London
EC2A 3DQ
UK

Printed in Hong Kong

Editor: Peter Darman
Picture research: Antony Shaw
Design: Dax Fullbrook
Production: Matt Weyland

Printed in Hong Kong

CONTENTS

9MM OWEN

SPECIFICATIONS

9MM OWEN

Type:
submachine gun

Calibre:
9mm (0.354in) Parabellum

Length:
0.813m (32in)

Length of barrel:
0.25m (9.85in)

Weight:
4kg (8.8lb)

Muzzle velocity:
419m (1375ft) per second

Feed:
33-round detachable box magazine (680–700rpm)

The Machine Carbine, 9mm Owen was a submachine gun designed by Lt Evelyn Owen, and entered production at Newcastle, New South Wales, in the course of November 1940. The weapon remained in production until September 1944, by which time some 45,000 guns had been produced. In service, the Owen soon showed itself to be a reliable and effective, and therefore popular, weapon. The bolt was protected against water, mud and dirt, which was a decided boon in the conditions prevalent in the Pacific theatres in which Australian troops fought, and in basic construction the weapon was very sturdy.

The feature that most easily differentiated the Owen from other submachine guns of the period was its vertical overhead magazine, a feature that provided for reliable feed and also made it easier for troops to use when lying on the ground. There were three primary variants of the Owen submachine gun: the Owen Mk I/42 was identifiable by the cooling fins on its barrel, the Owen Mk I/43 (specification at left) that was lightened by the omission of the cooling fins, and the Owen Mk I/44 that could be fitted with a bayonet. All three variants had an easily changed barrel secured by a quick-release plunger. There was also an Owen Mk II version, but this did not enter production.

MG 1907/12

The first Schwarzlose machine guns were manufactured during 1905 by the Steyr company in what was then the Austro-Hungarian Empire. Unique in being the only machine gun based on the retarded blow-back operating system, the Schwarzlose was very heavy and was sturdily constructed, and as a result of the operating system had only a comparatively short barrel generally fitted with a conical flash hider. The weapon was so over-engineered that many of its components seemed never to need replacement, and on the outbreak of World War II in 1939 large numbers of these weapons were still in service in many parts of Europe. Reliable operation of the earlier models was dependant on the use of oiled cartridges, but the need for this aspect was later eliminated, and the Schwarzlose appeared in many forms. The main variants were the Maschinengewehr Modelle 07 and the 08, but these were later brought up to the same standard as the MG 07/12. Variants (with revised designation when drafted into German service) in service during 1939 were the Austrian 8mm MG Modell 07/12 (s MG 7/12[oe]), Bulgarian 8mm, Dutch 7.9mm Mitrailleur M08 (s MG 241[h]), Mitrailleur M08/13 (s MG 242[h]) and Mitrailleur M08/15 (s MG 244[h]), Greek 6.5mm M12 (s MG 202[g]), Hungarian 8mm 07/12 (7/31), Italian 8mm 07/12 (s MG 267[i]), Romanian 6.5mm 07/12 and Yugoslav 7.9mm Mitralez M07/12S (s MG 247[j]).

SPECIFICATIONS

MG 1907/12

Type:
heavy water-cooled machine gun

Calibre:
8mm (0.315in)

Length:
1.066m (42in)

Length of barrel:
0.526m (20.75in)

Weight:
19.9kg (44lb) for gun and 19.8kg (43.75lb) for tripod

Muzzle velocity:
620m (2034ft) per second

Feed:
250-round fabric belt (400rpm)

FN HIGH POWER

SPECIFICATIONS

FN HIGH POWER

Type:
  semi-automatic pistol

Calibre:
  9mm (0.354in) Parabellum

Length:
  0.197m (7.75in)

Length of barrel:
  0.118m (4.65in)

Weight:
  1.01kg (2.44lb) loaded

Muzzle velocity:
  351m (1150ft) per second

Feed:
  13-round detachable box magazine

A design dating from 1925, the FN (Browning) modèle GP or GP35 was the last pistol created by John Browning before his death and remains one of the best pistols ever produced. The High-Power design owed little to earlier Browning pistols and incorporated a positive breech lock.

The construction was very sturdy, and an unusual feature was the 13-round magazine, which resulted in a bulky but still easily holdable butt. FN's licensed production began in 1935, and the pistol was produced for the Belgian, Dutch, Danish, Lithuanian and Romanian forces. Just before Belgium's fall to Germany in May 1940, the drawings were taken to the UK and then transferred to the John Inglis Company of Toronto, Canada, where further production followed for China and then Canada and the UK. The Canadian model was slightly different from the Belgian pistol, and had no provision for the fitting of a wooden holster stock to the butt. In British and Canadian service the GP35 was the Pistol, Browning, FN, 9mm HP No. 1 Mks 1 and 1*, and No 2 Mks 1 and 1*. Further manufacture in Belgium under German control resulted in a pistol known as the 9mm Pistole 640(b). Amazingly, or perhaps not given its excellent design and build, this weapon is still in service around the world.

FN 1924

Belgium's main constructor of small arms, the *Fabrique Nationale d'Armes de Guerre* located in Herstal, licence-manufactured Mauser bolt-action rifles from 1889 for the Belgian Army and also for export. From 1919, the year after Germany's defeat in World War I, FN built an updated and shortened version of the definitive Mauser Gewehr 1898 rifle as the Fusil Mauser FN, modèle 1924, which provided FN with one of its greatest export successes. The modèle 1924 was so closely similar to the Karabiner 98k that after Belgium's 1940 defeat by Germany the FN production facility needed only very modest changes to produce this later German rifle. The modèle 1924 was initially offered in 7, 7.65 and 7.9mm calibres. Together with the only marginally different modèles 1924/30 and 1930, the modèle 1924 was sold to many countries including, amongst World War II's combatants, Brazil, China, Greece, Lithuania, Luxembourg and Yugoslavia. The last established its own production facility to manufacture the modèle 24 as the Puska 7.9mm M 24, which paved the way for two slightly shortened variants, the Sokol-Puska 7.9mm and the Komitern Puska 7.9mm. Belgium did not adopt the modèle 24 until 1939, and the few such weapons captured by the Germans were designated Gewehr 220(b) with a prefix indicating the calibre.

SPECIFICATIONS

FN 1924

Type:
bolt-action rifle

Calibre:
7, 7.65 and 7.92mm (0.276, 0.301 and 0.312in)

Length:
1.10m (43in)

Length of barrel:
0.589m (23.2in)

Weight:
3.85kg (8.5lb) without bayonet

Muzzle velocity:
750m (2461ft) per second with 7.5mm ammunition

Feed:
5-round box magazine

ROSS RIFLE MK III

SPECIFICATIONS

ROSS RIFLE MK III

Type:
bolt-action rifle

Calibre:
7.7mm (0.303in)

Length:
1.285m (50.56in)

Length of barrel:
0.775m (30.15in)

Weight:
4.48kg (9.75lb)

Muzzle velocity:
792m (2600ft) per second

Feed:
5-round box magazine

The first Ross rifle was manufactured in 1896, and in the period up to 1915 there were many development and service models. The primary model in service after 1914 was the Model 1910, known to the British Army as the Rifle, Magazine, Ross, Mk IIIB, and to the Canadians as the Rifle, Ross, Mk III. From 1916 – when the Short Magazine Lee Enfield was adopted in its place after the Canadian weapon had been shown by experience in the trench warfare of World War I to lack adequate strength and reliability – the Ross rifle was relegated from standard infantry frontline use, although it was still used with considerable success as a sniping rifle, often fitted with a telescopic sight.

In the period between the world wars examples of the Ross rifle were exported to Lithuania, and then passed into Soviet hands after the USSR's 1939 seizure of the Baltic states. During 1940 some 70,000 Ross rifles were sold to the UK by the USA, which had bought an initial 20,000 such rifles in 1917 for training in the USA. The majority of these rifles was allocated to the Home Guard, but some weapons were released to fishing boat and small merchant ship crews to provide a very limited anti-aircraft defence capability. A few Ross rifles were issued to second-line units of the British Army at a time when Britain was desperate for weapons.

ZK VZ.383

Otherwise known as the ZK 383, the ZK vz.383 was a Czechoslovakian submachine gun, which was designed in 1933 at Brno by Josef and Frantisek Koucky, and entered production in the same factory shortly after that time. The weapon was retained in manufacture right through to 1948, three years after the end of World War II. The reason for this was that the ZK vz.383 was a notably well designed and capably manufactured weapon. The gun was distinguished by a number of unusual features, these including a 0.17kg (0.375lb) weight that could be added to the bolt to slow the rate of fire, a folding bipod (discarded on the ZK vz.383P model for paramilitary service) under the barrel and, on the post-war ZK vz.383H model, a folding magazine.

Another feature that enhanced the capabilities of the ZK vz.383 was a quick-change mechanism for the barrel. The Czechoslovak Army adopted the ZK vz.383 as its standard sub-machine gun in 1933, and weapons of this useful type were also exported to Bulgaria as well as a number of South American countries, but after Germany's two-part seizure of Czechoslovakia in 1938 and 1939 the weapon remained in production to meet the requirements of the Waffen-SS. Most of the submachine guns manufactured in World War II bore the designation vz.9.

SPECIFICATIONS

ZK VZ.383

Type:
submachine gun

Calibre:
9mm (0.354in) Parabellum

Length:
0.90m (35.4in)

Length of barrel:
0.325m (12.8in)

Weight:
4.27kg (9.4lb)

Muzzle velocity:
380m (1247ft) per second

Feed:
30-round detachable box magazine (500–700rpm)

ZB VZ/26

SPECIFICATIONS

ZB VZ/26

Type:
light air-cooled machine gun

Calibre:
7.92mm (0.312in)

Length:
1.161m (45.75in)

Barrel length:
0.672m (23.7in)

Weight:
9.6kg (21.3lb)

Muzzle velocity:
760m (2493ft) per second

Feed:
20- or 30-round detachable box magazine (550rpm)

The *Ceskoslovenska Zbrojovka* company, located at Brno (Brunn) in Czechoslovakia, was created in 1922, soon after the country's emergence after the end of World War I as an independent state out of the wreckage of the Austro-Hungarian Empire, and its first product was the Praga Model 24 belt-fed light machine gun designed by Vaclav Holek. A magazine-fed model was introduced some two years later as the ZB vz/26. This was an excellently designed and sturdily manufactured gun of the gas-operated type, and soon proved itself popular as it was exported to several parts of the world. The Czechoslovak Army ordered the type as its standard light machine gun, and these weapons were impressed by Germany after its 1939 seizure of that part of Czechoslovakia still left after the Munich agreement of 1938. Many countries secured licensed manufacturing agreements for the vz/26. The ZB vz/27 differed from the vz/26 only in small details, and further development led to the ZB vz/30 and thence, via the interim ZB vz/33, the British Bren Gun. The main versions of the vz/26 were the Czechoslovak 7.92mm Kulomet vz/26 (le MG 26[t]), Soviet 7.92mm Rutschnoi pulemet obrazets 1926 (le MG 146/2[r]) and Yugoslav 7.92mm Puska-Mitralez 7.9mm M26 Brunn (le MG 146/1[j]). Other users were China, Japan, Lithuania, Romania, Spain, Sweden and Turkey.

MADSEN

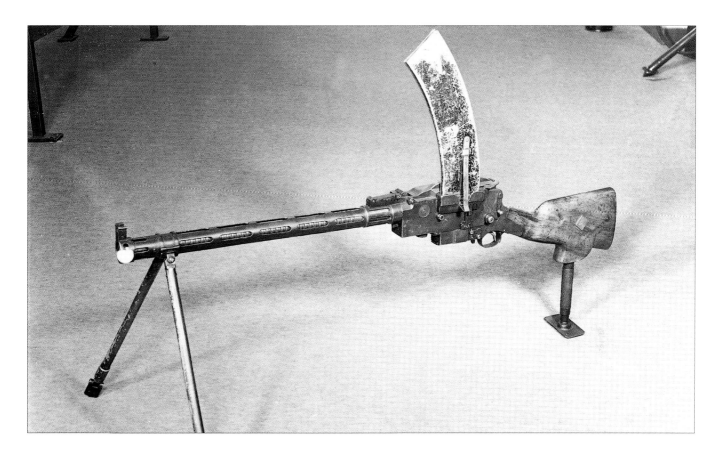

The first model of the Madsen light machine gun appeared during 1904, and the series then remained in production into the late 1950s in a large number of models and indeed calibres for export to many parts of the world. It is difficult to see why the Madsen light machine gun was a notable sales success as it was expensive and offered high capability in no particular respect, but the weapons were certainly well made and excellently engineered. Germany maintained production during its occupation of Denmark between 1940 and 1945. Many of the Dutch guns were seized by the Japanese during their conquest of the Dutch East Indies. The main variants used in World War II (with the German designation in parentheses where applicable) were the British 0.303in M1915, 1919, 1929, 1931 and 1939 (see specification); Bulgarian 8mm M1915, 1924 and 1927; Chinese 7.92mm M1916, 1930 and 1937; Danish 8mm Rekytgevaer M1903/24 (8mm le MG 158[d]), Rekytgevaer M1924 (8mm le MG 159[d]) and Rekytgevaer Madsen 8mm (s MG 258[d]); Dutch 6.5mm M1919, 1923, 1926, 1927, 1934, 1938 and 1939; Estonian 0.303in M1925 and 1937; Finnish 7.62mm M1910, 1920, 1921 and 1923; French 8mm M1915, 1919, 1922 and 1924 (8mm le MG 157[f]); German 7.92mm M1941 and 1942 (7.92mm MG [Madsen]); and Hungarian 7.92mm M1925 and 1943.

SPECIFICATIONS

MADSEN

Type:
light air-cooled machine gun

Calibre:
7.7mm (0.303in)

Length:
1.143m (45in)

Barrel length:
0.584m (23in)

Weight:
9.07kg (20lb)

Muzzle velocity:
715m (2346ft) per second

Feed:
20-, 25-, 30- and 40-round box magazines (450rpm)

KONEPISTOOLI M/31

SPECIFICATIONS

KONEPISTOOLI M/31

Type:
submachine gun

Calibre:
9mm (0.354in) Parabellum

Length:
0.87m (34.25in)

Length of barrel:
0.3175m (12.5in)

Weight:
4.68kg (10.3lb)

Muzzle velocity:
400m (1312ft) per second

Feed:
20-, 50- and 71-round box or drum magazine (450rpm)

The family of Finnish submachine guns universally known as the "Suomi" was developed from 1922, resulting in the Koonepistooli m/26 as the first production model. This was chambered for the 7.63mm Mauser round, but in 1931 the m/31 was produced for the altogether superior 9mm Parabellum round. The m/1931 was one of the most far-reaching submachine gun designs ever created, and strongly influenced Soviet design thinking.

A capably designed and well-manufactured weapon, the m/31 was made under licence in Denmark, Sweden and Switzerland, as well as being produced in Finland for national use as well as export to countries such as Norway. By submachine gun standards the m/31 was both expensive and heavy as all of its major parts were machined from solid metal, but the weapon was notably accurate as a result of its long barrel. Madsen produced for Danish service the M42, which was later taken over by the Germans as the 9mm Maschinenpistole 746(d). The main problem with submachine guns in general was their accuracy and ammunition usage. In battle troops tended to fire bursts inaccurately, which, though it may have made them feel better, used a lot of ammunition for very little results. A division could use hundreds of thousands of rounds in a short space of time.

PISTOLE M1935

For reasons possibly of reliability but probably of tradition, the French Army was slow to consider and adopt the automatic pistol as a replacement for the revolver. When the service did opt for such a weapon, so unprepared for the switch was the French armaments industry that the service had initially to use a variety of Spanish weapons. Thus it was only in 1935 that the French Army fixed on its first automatic pistol of indigenous design by Charles Fetter of SACM, and this became the Pistole Automatique modèle 1935A.

The modèle 1935A was clearly derived from the Colt M1911A1 with modest changes in the recoil spring and locking mechanism as well as a different cartridge, the 7.65mm Long, only rarely used outside France. This fact severely hindered the possibility of export sales, and in fact the modèle 1935A was used only by France. The modèle 1935A was complemented by its modèle 1935S subvariant optimized for easier manufacture. The modèle 1935S was characterized by a straighter butt, revisions to the locking mechanism, and a muzzle extending slightly from the slide. The modèles 1935A and 1935S (specification at right) were both in service at the time of France's June 1940 defeat by Germany, which subsequently adopted both weapons with the designation 7.65mm Pistole 625(f).

SPECIFICATIONS

PISTOLE M1935

Type:
semi-automatic piston

Calibre:
7.65mm (0.301in) Long

Length:
0.188m (7.4in)

Length of barrel:
0.104m (4.1in)

Weight:
0.79kg (1.75lb)

Muzzle velocity:
345m (1132ft) per second

Feed:
8-round box magazine

FUSIL M1916

SPECIFICATIONS

FUSIL M1916

Type:
bolt-action rifle

Calibre:
8mm (0.315in)

Length:
1.306m (51.4in)

Length of barrel:
0.797m (31.4in)

Weight:
4.2kg (9.25lb)

Muzzle velocity:
725m (2379ft) per second

Feed:
5-round fixed box magazine

By the middle of World War I the French Army had come to the belated recognition that the Mannlicher type of three-round fixed magazine (loaded with individual rounds) used by the Fusil modèle 07/15 was a severe tactical limitation, and therefore ordered the revision of this otherwise good weapon with a larger magazine loaded by means of a five-round charger. The resulting weapon was the Fusil d'Infanterie modèle 1916 (specifications in table left), which was most readily identifiable by the fact that the magazine now extended below the handguard.

After World War I large numbers of modèle 1916 rifles were delivered to many of France's European allies, most notably Greece, Poland, Romania and Yugoslavia, as well as ex-enemy Turkey. By 1939 only France and Yugoslavia were still using the weapon, and after Germany's 1940 and 1941 victories over these countries captured weapons were absorbed into the German inventory with the designations Gewehr 304(f) and, in the case of the Yugoslav Puska 8mm M16F, Gewehr 304(j). A carbine version of the Fusil modèle 1916 was also produced as the Mousqueton modèle 1916, upgraded in 1927 to modèle 16/27 standard. This weapon was exported to Romania and Yugoslavia, the latter using the type as the Karabini 8mm M16F.

FUSIL M07/1915

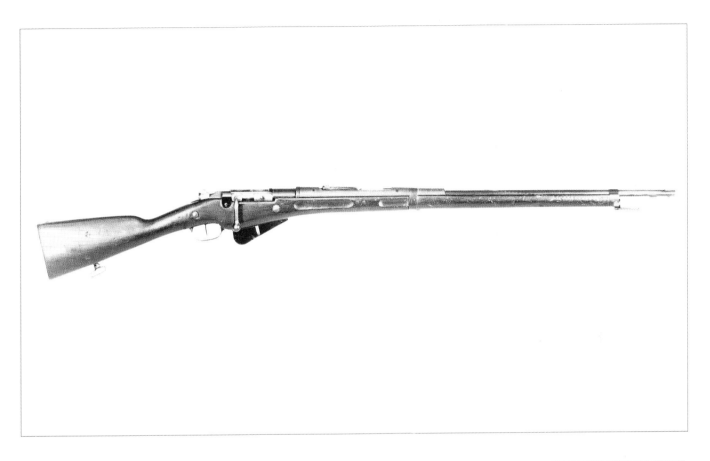

The designation Fusil d'Infanterie modèle 1907 transformé 1915 et modifié 1934 was the official name of the weapon that was a radical upgrade of the modèle 07/15, and was often called the Fusil modèle 1934 or Fusil modèle 07/15 M34.

This weapon was created in 1934 by shortening the modèle 07/15 and installing a new barrel to fire the 7.5mm Cartouche modèle 29 rimless round, which was now loaded into a five-round magazine of the Mauser pattern. The weapon that resulted from this process bore only a limited resemblance to the modèle 07/15 weapon, but despite being an altogether improved type, was not produced in large enough numbers to replace all the examples of the older rifle. Production of the modèle 07/15 M34 ended in 1940, by which time only part of the French Army had received the weapon. The total defeat at the hands of Nazi Germany in June 1940 naturally halted the army's weapons modernization programme.

The Germans, as with other weapons, took extant models into their own inventory with the designation Gewehr 241(f). It is worth noting that there was also a cavalry version of this rifle, and that this differed from the infantry weapon only in having a turned-down, rather than projecting-bolt, handle.

SPECIFICATIONS

FUSIL M07/1915

Type:
bolt-action rifle

Calibre:
7.5mm (0.295in)

Length:
1.084m (42.7in)

Length of barrel:
0.58m (22.8in)

Weight:
3.56kg (7.85lb)

Muzzle velocity:
825m (2707ft) per second

Feed:
5-round fixed box magazine

FUSIL MAS 36

SPECIFICATIONS

FUSIL MAS 36

Type:
bolt-action rifle

Calibre:
7.5mm (0.295in)

Length:
1.019m (40.13in)

Length of barrel:
0.574m (22.6in)

Weight:
3.67kg (8.29lb)

Muzzle velocity:
825m (2707ft) per second

Feed:
5-round fixed box magazine

When the French Army switched from the 8mm Lebel rimmed to 7.5mm rimless cartridge in 1924 (Cartouche modèle 1924 later upgraded to Cartouche modèle 1929), it decided that the time was ripe for a new rifle created specifically to use the new cartridge. A prototype weapon appeared in 1932, but it was 1936 before the definitive Fusil MAS 36 was adopted. In many ways the MAS 36 could be regarded as an obsolescent weapon even at the time of its introduction, for by this time many armies were introducing or at least developing semi-automatic rifles. However, the French opted in the MAS 36 for bolt action, specifically of a modified Mauser type (with the locking lugs at the back of the receiver instead of the bolt head) and an awkward bolt handle angled forward and downwards. In common with other French rifles, the MAS 36 lacked any safety catch. The MAS 36 was the last bolt-action rifle adopted by a major power, and by 1939 and the outbreak of World War II full production was in hand at the *Manufacture d'Armes de Saint-Etienne*. After France's 1940 surrender, the Germans took over enough rifles to equip several of the divisions of its occupation force with what now became the Gewehr 242(f). Produced only in small numbers, the MAS 36 CR39 development of the MAS 36 for paratroops featured a folding aluminium butt.

HOTCHKISS M1909

Arguably the first genuine light machine gun to enter large-scale service anywhere in the world, the Fusil Mitrailleur Hotchkiss modèle 1909 was often called the "Benet-Mercier", and was based on features employed in the larger Hotchkiss machine guns, including the gas-operated mechanism and the feed by a metal strip that in the case of the modèle 1909 was inverted and often resulted in feed problems. During World War I the modèle 1909 was widely used by the French, and also delivered to the UK and USA. Improved Hotchkiss light machine guns were the modèle 1922 and heavy-barrel modèle 1926, both of which could have feed mechanisms other than the usual Hotchkiss strip. By the outbreak of World War II France and the USA had disposed of their weapons, but the UK kept limited numbers for airfield defence. Modèle 1909 weapons captured by the Germans included the British 0.303in Gun, Machine, Hotchkiss, Mks I and I* (7.7mm le MG 136[e] and le MG 136[g] taken from the British and Greeks), and modèles 1922 and 1926, including the French 6.5mm Fusil Mitrailleur Hotchkiss modèle 1922 (6.5mm le MG 105[f]) and 8mm Fusil Mitrailleur Hotchkiss modèle 1926 (8mm le MG 105[f]), Greek 6.5mm Hotchkiss Model 1926 (6.5mm le MG 104[g], 7.9mm Hotchkiss Model 1926 (7.9mm le MG 152/1[g]), and Hotchkiss Model 1926 (7.9mm le MG 152/2[g]).

SPECIFICATIONS

HOTCHKISS M1909

Type:
light air-cooled machine gun

Calibre:
7.92mm (0.312in)

Length:
1.22m (48in)

Length of barrel:
0.55m (21.65in)

Weight:
9kg (19.8lb)

Muzzle velocity:
745m (2444ft) per second

Feed:
25-round metal strip (500rpm)

HOTCHKISS M1914

SPECIFICATIONS

HOTCHKISS M1914

Type:
medium air-cooled machine gun

Calibre:
8mm (0.315in)

Length:
1.27m (50in)

Length of barrel:
0.775m (30.5in)

Weight:
23.6kg (52lb) excluding tripod

Muzzle velocity:
725m (2379ft) per second

Feed:
24- or 30-round strips, or 249-round belt (400–600rpm)

The first Hotchkiss machine guns entered French service in 1897, and from the next year the weapon was also exported. These modèles 1897 and 1898 were duly followed by the Mitrailleuse Hotchkiss modèles 1910 and 1914 weapons. All four were similar in their use of a gas-powered operating system, a heavy barrel with five large cooling rings, and the Hotchkiss metal strip feed arrangement. This last was a limiting feature because it limited burst lengths to a maximum of 40 rounds, so the modèle 1914 introduced a type of belt feed in which three-round "mini-strips" were connected into 249-round "belts". Well made and reliable, the Hotchkiss machine gun was produced in large numbers and, for the export market, in a variety of calibres. However, the Hotchkiss guns were heavy and bulky. Thus by 1939 most surviving weapons were used in the static role as defensive weapons. The Germans captured large numbers of weapons and placed them in German service: the Belgian 7.65mm Mitrailleuse "Hotchkiss" (7.65mm s MG 220[b]), French 8mm Mitrailleuse Hotchkiss modèle 1914 (8mm s MG 257[f]), Norwegian 6.5mm Hotchkiss mitralose m/98 (6.5mm s MG 201[n]) and Hotchkiss's 7.9mm mitralose m/98t (7.9mm s MG 240[n]), and Polish 7.9mm Karabin maszynowy Hotchkiss (14/25) (7.9mm s MG 238[p]).

HOTCHKISS M1930

During 1930 Hotchkiss introduced a larger-calibre version of its 11mm modèle de ballon anti-observation balloon machine gun of 1917 as the Mitrailleuse Hotchkiss de 13mm 2 modèle 1930. This looked like a scaled-up British Bren Gun and was fed by an 30-round overhead box magazine of curved shape, as dictated by the use of rimmed ammunition. The modèle 1930 was schemed for capability in a number of roles, with optimization in a given role provided by the gun's different mountings.

The three main variants were the Affût d'accompagnement à roues à une mitrailleuse Hotchkiss de 13mm 2 de cavalerie for infantry use on two spoked wheels and with a small limber for ammunition and spares, the Affût-trepied leger de cavalerie à une mitrailleuse Hotchkiss de 13mm 2 for cavalry use on a tripod, and the Affût-trepied R3 à deux mitrailleuses Hotchkiss de 13mm 2 for anti-aircraft use with two machine guns on a heavy tripod mounting with a complex sight. The modèle 1930 was exported in small numbers to Greece, Poland, Romania, the USSR and Yugoslavia, and was copied in Japan as the Type 93. Germany used captured French weapons with the designation 13.2mm MG 271(f). All in all, the Hotchkiss was an average weapon.

SPECIFICATIONS

HOTCHKISS M1930

Type:
heavy air-cooled machine gun

Calibre:
13.2mm (0.519in)

Length:
2.41m (95in)

Length of barrel:
1.65m (65in)

Weight:
37.5kg (87lb)

Muzzle velocity:
700m (2297ft) per second

Feed:
30-round box magazine (250–300rpm)

CHATELLERAULT

SPECIFICATIONS

CHATELLERAULT

Type:
light air-cooled machine gun

Calibre:
7.5mm (0.295in)

Length:
1.007m (39.65in)

Length of barrel:
0.50m (19.7in)

Weight:
8.93kg (19.7lb)

Muzzle velocity:
820m (2690ft) per second

Feed:
25-round detachable box magazine (450–600rpm)

Created as a light machine gun to supplant the unsatisfactory Chauchat in French service, the Fusil Mitrailleur Chatellerault modèle 1924 was a useful weapon based conceptually on an American weapon, the Browning Automatic Rifle, but with unusual features including two triggers: the front and rear triggers controlled single-shot and automatic fire respectively. The weapon and its specially designed round entered service before full development had been completed, however, and as a result there were a number of accidents including some caused by bursting barrels. Full development resulted in the modèle 1924/29, which was the French Army's standard light machine gun at the start of World War II.

The modèle 1924/29 was a first-rate weapon, and the Germans took captured examples into their own inventory with the designation 7.5mm le MG 116(f), while a few modèle 1924 weapons became 7.5mm le MG 115(f) guns. Developed from the modèle 1924/29 for use in fixed defences and armoured fighting vehicles, the Mitrailleuse de 7.5mm modèle 1931 had a butt of odd contours and was fed with ammunition from a 150-round drum magazine mounted on the left-hand side of the weapon. The Germans used this machine gun in the anti-aircraft role with the designation 7.5mm Kpfw MG 331(f).

PISTOLE 08

Generally known as the "Luger", the Pistole 08 is amongst the most celebrated pistols ever placed in production. The first Luger pistols for military service were manufactured in 1900 to meet a Swiss order, and the type was also adopted by the German navy during 1904 and then by the German Army in 1908. It was this last order that led to the designation P 08, which became the most important of some 35 or more Luger pistol variants. The P 08 was the standard German service pistol until 1938, when the P 38 was introduced as its successor, but even so the P 08 remained in production to 1943 and at the end of World War II in 1945 remained in full service for lack of adequate numbers of the P 38. Oddly enough, the P 08 was not a first-class weapon for military use as it was susceptible to jamming when its open toggle mechanism was clogged by dirt. On the other side of the coin, however, the P 08 was a very "pointable" weapon and was therefore fairly accurate. The most common P 08 version had a 0.103m (4.06in) barrel, but the barrel of the naval model was 0.152m (6in) long. Other than Germany, countries that used the P 08 included Abyssinia, Bulgaria, Finland, Latvia, the Netherlands, Persia, Portugal, Romania, Switzerland and Turkey: the Dutch weapons were produced in the UK by Vickers during the early 1920s.

SPECIFICATIONS

PISTOLE 08

Type:
semi-automatic pistol

Calibre:
9mm (0.354in) Parabellum

Length:
0.222m (8.75in)

Length of barrel:
0.103m (4.06in)

Weight:
0.876kg (1.93lb)

Muzzle velocity:
320m (1050ft) per second

Feed:
8-round detachable straight box magazine

WALTHER PP

SPECIFICATIONS

WALTHER PP

Type:
semi-automatic pistol

Calibre:
7.65 or 9mm (0.301 or 0.354in)

Length:
0.162m (6.38in)

Length of barrel:
0.085m (3.35in)

Weight:
0.708kg (1.56lb)

Muzzle velocity:
290m (951ft) per second with 7.65mm ammunition

Feed:
8-round detachable straight box magazine

A semi-automatic pistol that was first delivered in 1929, the Walther Model PP had been designed for police use as indicated by its full designation, Polizei Pistole (police pistol). The pistol used the Walther double-action trigger mechanism that was also used on the later P 38, and other features included a lightweight receiver and, next to the hammer, a signal button that protruded when the weapon was loaded.

In overall terms the design was light and slim. From 1939 the Model PP was manufactured for military service in 7.65mm and 9mm calibres, the main operators being the German Air Force (Luftwaffe) and the German Army's tank (panzer) arm, both of which needed a small weapon. Introduced in 1931, the Model PPK was a smaller version of the Model PP and was initially manufactured for easy carriage by plain clothes policemen as indicated by the full designation, Polizei Pistole Kriminal (criminal police pistol).

Except for its smaller size, the Model PPK was similar to the Model PP and was delivered for service use (especially by the German Air Force) from 1939. The Model PPK was chambered for the same calibre as the Model PP, the magazine holding seven 7.65mm or six 9mm rounds. Like most German small arms, the PP was manufactured to a high standard.

WALTHER P38

The Pistole 38, another semi-automatic weapon from the Walther stable, entered service with the German armed forces in 1938 as successor to the P 08. It embodied a double-action trigger mechanism developed from the earlier Models PP and PPK, and also featured the signal pin which extended beside the hammer when there was a round in the chamber. The P 38 was mechanically reliable and in service was a popular weapon, being able to withstand extremes of temperature and inhospitable terrain (especially in the USSR), but was never produced in numbers large enough to allow complete replacement of the P 08. Manufacture was undertaken in Belgium and Bohemia-Moravia (occupied Czechoslovakia) as well as in Germany itself.

There were a number of production subvariants, each differing from the baseline model only in small details, before the P 38 was taken out of production in 1945, and although the weapon's manufacture became cruder as World War II progressed (a result of raw material shortages that affected the whole of the German armaments industry), the P 38 was always reliable. Indeed, so useful was the type that it was later placed back in production to meet the requirements of the army of the Federal German Republic.

SPECIFICATIONS

WALTHER P38

Type:
semi-automatic pistol

Calibre:
9mm (0.354in) Parabellum

Length:
0.2185m (8.6in)

Length of barrel:
0.1245m (4.9in)

Weight:
0.95kg (2.1lb)

Muzzle velocity:
340m (1115ft) per second

Feed:
8-round detachable straight box magazine

KARABINER 98K

SPECIFICATIONS

KARABINER 98K

Type:
  bolt-action rifle

Calibre:
  7.92mm (0.312in)

Length:
  1.1075m (43.6in)

Length of barrel:
  0.739m (23.6in)

Weight:
  3.9kg (8.6lb)

Muzzle velocity:
  755m (2477ft) per second

Feed:
  5-round fixed box magazine

In World War I the German Army decided that its standard rifle, the Gewehr 98, was too long for effective use. There was little that could be done at the time, but by 1924 Mauser had developed a rifle shorter than its Gewehr 98 and based on its "Standard" model for export sales: this was manufactured in Belgium and other countries, but did not enter German production until 1935 as the Karabiner 98k (the letter suffix standing for *kurz*, or short). German production resulted in the delivery of millions of these weapons before 1945, and numbers were further boosted by manufacture in Belgium and Bohemia-Moravia (occupied Czechoslovakia). As was inevitable in a programme of this size and duration, there were a number of variations in length, weight and furniture: late-production Kar 98k weapons, for instance, lacked any bayonet lug. Service experience confirmed that the Kar 98k was both sturdy and accurate, but also that the small capacity of the five-round magazine was a tactical disadvantage. Another rifle based on the "Standard" Mauser rifle was the 7.92mm Model Chiang Kai-shek, or "Generalissimo", that was introduced in 1935 and was to all intents and purposes identical to the Kar 98k. Another close relative of the Kar 98k was the Belgian 7.65mm Fusil modèle 35 that was later taken into German service as the Gewehr 262(b).

GEWEHR 41

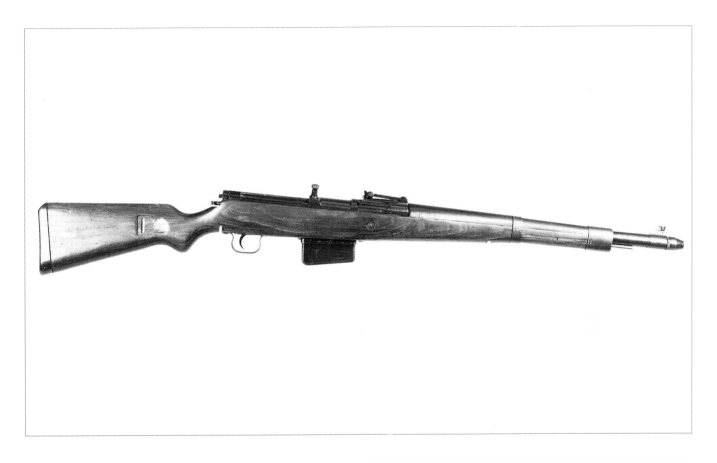

In 1940 the Germany Army, currently equipped with bolt-action weapons so far as rifles and carbines were concerned, issued a requirement for a semi-automatic (or self-loading) rifle to succeeded the various Mauser weapons of the Gewehr 98 series. The requirement elicited very similar designs from Mauser and Walther, and the German authorities ordered prototypes of each type for competitive evaluation before any major production contracts were placed. Mauser's Gewehr 41(M) rapidly revealed itself to be inadequate for service, while Walther's Gewehr 41(W) (see specifications) received the order. The Gew 41(W) was based on virtually the same gas-operated mechanism as the Gew 41(M), namely a variant of a Danish system. This Bang system trapped muzzle gases and diverted them rearward to power a piston that operated the ejection/loading mechanism. As well as being difficult to produce, the Gew 41(W) was not an operational success for it was difficult to load quickly and its complicated mechanism led to an unacceptably low level of reliability. Other limitations were the weapon's considerable weight and also a design that made the weapon unhandy. Production was terminated after the advent of the Gewehr 43, but the type remained in service to the end of World War II, being used mainly on the Eastern Front.

SPECIFICATIONS

GEWEHR 41

Type:
semi-automatic rifle

Calibre:
7.92mm (0.312in)

Length:
1.175m (46.25in)

Length of barrel:
0.5525m (21.75in)

Weight:
5.1kg (11.25lb)

Muzzle velocity:
775m (2543ft) per second

Feed:
10-round fixed straight box magazine

GEWEHR 43

SPECIFICATIONS

GEWEHR 43

Type:
 semi-automatic rifle

Calibre:
 7.92mm (0.312in)

Length:
 1.117m (44in)

Length of barrel:
 0.55m (21.6in)

Weight:
 4.4kg (9.56lb)

Muzzle velocity:
 775m (2543ft) per second

Feed:
 10-round detachable straight box magazine

When they evaluated the Tokarev semi-automatic rifle, of which they captured numerous examples in 1941 and 1942, the Germans quickly appreciated that the Soviet gas-operated system offered several advantages over the modified Bang system used in their Gewehr 41 weapons. It was seen that the Russian gas-operated mechanism had many advantages over the system used on the Gew 41. The Gew 41(W) was already in production, but the Germans now modified the action to a system modelled closely on that of the Soviet self-loading rifle to create the Gewehr 43 firing the German Army's standard 7.92mm cartridge. Initial tests confirmed that the Gew 43 was an altogether better weapon than the Gew 41(W), offering much greater reliability under all operating conditions, and the new type replaced the Gew 41(W) in production. The new self-loading rifle was simpler, and therefore quicker and cheaper, to manufacture, and the opportunity was taken to introduce features such as a reduction in machined components, an increase in forged parts, laminated rather than solid wooden furniture, and a detachable magazine that could be loaded with two standard five-round clips. The weapon was completed with provision for the Zf41 telescopic sight as standard, and from 1944 there was also a Karabiner 43 version shortened by some 50mm (1.97in).

FG 42

The German paratroop arm was an element of the air force, and many of its weapons were therefore different from those of the army. Thus when the army issued its specification for an assault rifle, the air force decided not to adopt the 7.92mm *kurz* (short) intermediate-power round and therefore contracted with Rheinmetall-Borsig for an assault rifle suitable for airborne use and chambered for the original 7.92mm high-power round. The resulting Fallschirmjägergewehr 42 was one of the most remarkable weapons developed in World War II, for although there was nothing entirely novel, the FG 42 marked an evolutionary stage in the development of the compact assault rifle with a straight-through design. In some respects the FG 42 had affinities to the light machine gun, especially in features such as the permanently attached bipod that could be fixed at any point on the exposed barrel. Other notable elements of the design were the muzzle brake/compensator and the fixed folding bayonet, but a poor aspect was the lack of any provision for the barrel to be changed easily. The FG 42 was delivered in two main variants, one with a steel butt and a sloping pistol grip, and the other with a wooden butt and conventional grip. The weapon was expensive to manufacture, and as a result only 7000 were completed.

SPECIFICATIONS

FG 42

Type:
airborne forces assault rifle

Calibre:
7.92mm (0.312in)

Length:
0.94m (37in)

Length of barrel:
0.502m (19.75in)

Weight:
4.53kg (9.94lb)

Muzzle velocity:
760m (2493ft) per second

Feed:
20-round magazine (750–800rpm)

STURMGEWEHR 44

SPECIFICATIONS

STURMGEWEHR 44

Type:
assault rifle

Calibre:
7.92mm (0.312in)

Length:
0.94m (37in)

Length of barrel:
0.419m (16.5in)

Weight:
5.22kg (11.5lb)

Muzzle velocity:
650m (2,133ft) per second

Feed:
30-round detachable box magazine (500rpm)

Experience with the 8000 examples of the Haenel Maschinenkarabiner 42(H) assault rifle used for operational trials on the Eastern Front was generally successful, but indicated the need for changes whose implementation created the Maschinenpistole 43 firing the same 7.92mm *kurz* (short) intermediate-power round. The first MP 43s were delivered in 1943, and the type was retained in manufacture without noticeable change, except to facilitate production, right to the end of World War II. The MP 43/1 appeared late in 1943 and differed from the MP 43 only in its provision for the installation of a grenade-launcher cup at the muzzle. In 1944 the designation was changed to MP 44 for no apparent reason, although some MP 44 weapons had provision for a telescopic sight, and the definitive designation adopted late in 1944 was Sturmgewehr 44 or StG 44, an appellation selected for political rather than military reasons. The weapons of the MP 43 family were very effective, and may in fact be regarded as the first truly successful assault rifles that in many ways paved the way for assault rifle development after World War II. Among the accessories for the series were the Zielgerät 1229 "Vampir" infra-red night sight that appeared in small numbers during 1945, and the Krummlauf (curved leaf) barrel fitting and sight allowing the weapon to be fired round an angle of 30°.

MP 28/II

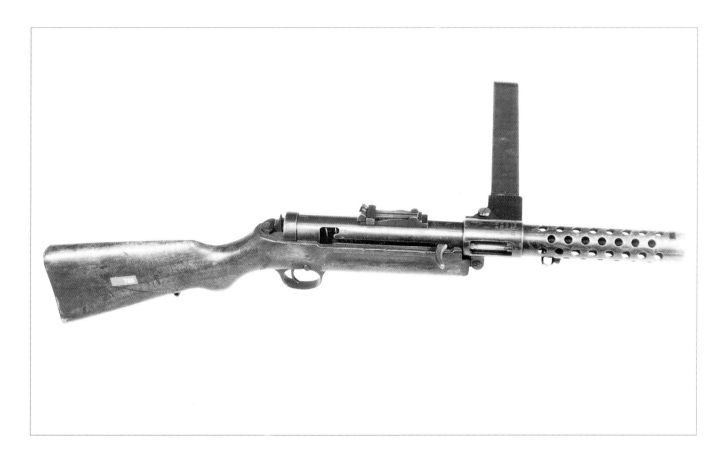

The Maschinenpistole 28/II sub-machine was in essence a 1928 development of the MP 18/I, which entered service in 1918 as the German Army's first such weapon, by Hugo Schmeisser for production by Haenel (interestingly, his name would be internationally associated with the later MP 38 and 40, though in fact he had very little to do with these weapons – the association is largely the result of Hollywood fantasy). The MP 28/II had a fire selector (single-shot or automatic) rather than the MP 18/I's automatic fire only, and less evident were a number of internal modifications. The type was produced as a commercial venture aimed at the export market, and was therefore produced in a number of calibres with particular features to suit the weapon to its various buyers. The weapon sold well to countries in South America, as well as to Belgium, China and Japan. The type was also made in Spain and Belgium (*Etablissements Anciens Pieper* at Herstal) as the Belgian Army's Mitraillette 34, and indeed many MP 28/II models were licence-made at Herstal for export. The MP 28/II saw extensive service in the Spanish Civil War, and after the outbreak of World War II in September 1939 all German production went to the German armed forces, which also used captured Belgian weapons after 1940 with the official designation MP 740(b).

SPECIFICATIONS

MP 28/II

Type:
submachine gun

Calibre:
9mm (0.354mm) Parabellum

Length:
0.81m (32in)

Length of barrel:
0.20m (7.9in)

Weight:
4kg (8.8lb)

Muzzle velocity:
380m (1247ft) per second

Feed:
20-, 32- 50-round detachable magazine (500rpm)

ERMA

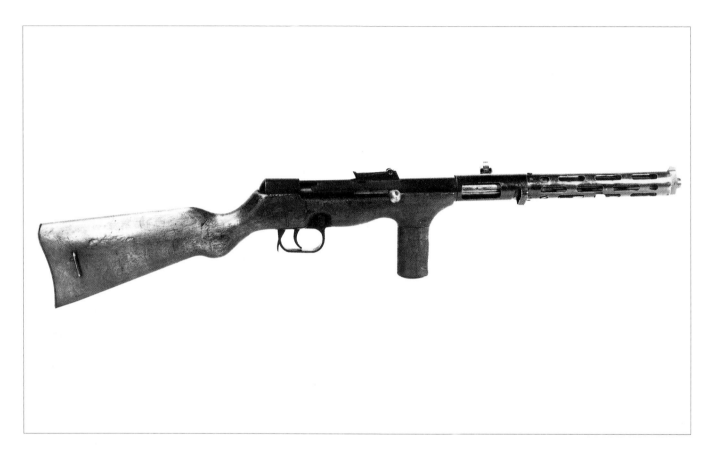

SPECIFICATIONS

ERMA

Type:
submachine gun

Calibre:
9mm (0.354in) Parabellum

Length:
0.90m (35.5in)

Length of barrel:
0.25m (9.9in)

Weight:
4.15kg (9.2lb)

Muzzle velocity:
380m (1247ft) per second

Feed:
20- or 32-round detachable box magazine (500rpm)

The Maschinenpistole Erma (or MPE) was designed in the early 1930s by Heinrich Vollmer for the Erfurter Maschinenfabrik company, hence the weapon's name. The Erma was a development of a Vollmer design of the mid-1920s, which featured a main spring enclosed in a telescopic tube to keep out dirt and other matter that might otherwise have jammed the action: this system became standard in subsequent German submachine guns such as the MP 38 and MP 40. Other features of the MPE were the extensive use of steel tube to reduce manufacturing time and cost, and the vertical wooden fore grip, although some of the weapons had a horizontal fore grip. The MPE appeared in time to be adopted for the German Army at the time of its initial expansion after the rise to power of the Nazi party in 1933, and remained a first-line German weapon until 1942, when surviving MPE submachine guns were relegated to second-line use. Modest numbers of MPE submachine guns were delivered to France for service with the official designation Pistolet Mitrailleur Vollmer Erma, and Yugoslavia also took the type in a variant with a lengthened barrel. The MPE was also manufactured in Spain and saw use in the Spanish Civil War. A subvariant manufactured in small quantities was a silenced model for the security police of the Vichy French regime operating under German supervision.

MP 38

The Maschinenpistole 38 is one of the most celebrated, or perhaps infamous, submachine guns ever placed in service. Designed by the Erma-Werke, the MP 38 introduced a number of unusual and innovative features: the main spring was contained within a telescopic sleeve (as pioneered in the limited-production MP Erma), the butt could be folded, and there was no wood in the weapon, which was therefore entirely of steel and plastic construction. Created from the outset for service with airborne and motorized troops (and thus with the folding butt), the MP 38 had a magazine located vertically under the weapon.

The MP 38 entered production in 1938 and was succeeded in 1940 by the MP 40. Combat experience with the MP 38 in Poland during September 1939 revealed the need for a safety mechanism on the cocking handle when this was in the forward (round cambered) position, when a knock could result in the weapon firing: thus a folding latch was added on the cocking handle to engage a notch on the receiver when forward, thus preventing any movement of the bolt. This created the MP38/40, and the feature was gradually added to most surviving MP 38 weapons after 1940. Contrary to popular belief, Hugo Schmeisser was never involved in the design of the weapon.

SPECIFICATIONS

MP 38

Type:
submachine gun

Calibre:
9mm (0.354in) Parabellum

Length:
0.833m (32.8in), butt extended

Length of barrel:
0.252m (9.9in)

Weight:
4.086kg (9lb)

Muzzle velocity:
380m (1247ft) per second

Feed:
32-round detachable box magazine (500rpm)

MP 40

SPECIFICATIONS

MP 40

Type:
submachine gun

Calibre:
9mm (0.354in) Parabellum

Length:
0.833m (32.8in), butt extended

Length of barrel:
0.252m (9.9in)

Weight:
4.027kg (8.88lb)

Muzzle velocity:
380m (1247ft) per second

Feed:
32-round detachable box magazine (500rpm)

The MP 38 was a technical and tactical success, but was also expensive to manufacture in terms of materials and time. The MP 38 was therefore re-designed as the Maschinenpistole 40 that was generally similar to the MP 38 but far easier to manufacture, as machining was reduced to a minimum and the use of welding and pressed components was maximized. As well as speeding production, these changes also made it possible for the MP 40 to be made by a larger number of companies drawing on the efforts of a pool of subcontractors delivering subassemblies. The MP 40 thus inaugurated the era of the swift and cheap manufacture of basic small arms, and was one of the most important submachine guns of World War II. Operational use of the weapon on the Eastern Front revealed that the MP 40 was not without its limitations, however, most notably by comparison with the Soviets' PPSh submachine gun that could be fitted with a 71-round drum magazine. This led to the creation of the MP 40/II that introduced a wider magazine housing to carry a side-by-side pair of MP 40 magazines: when the first magazine had been emptied, the complete assembly could be pushed over to bring the second magazine into position. The MP 40/II was delivered from 1943, but was not notably effective and was therefore manufactured only in modest numbers.

MP 41

Given the fact that far-sighted submachine guns such as the MP 38 and MP 40, with their all-metal construction and features to facilitate mass production, had clearly indicated the most practical line of development for such weapons under wartime conditions, the Maschinenpistole 41 could be seen only as something of an anachronism demanding somewhat greater manufacturing resources for a weapon that offered little operational advantage, something that Germany really could not afford given the industrial power of the enemies ranged against her.

The weapon was manufactured by Haenel on the basis of a development, by Hugo Schmeisser, of the MP 40. The MP 41 retained the barrel, bolt and operating mechanism of the MP 40 in combination with wooden furniture (including a full stock) derived conceptually from that of MP 28/II.

Neither the German armed forces not the police ordered the weapon, so it is uncertain why the type in fact entered production. As it was, only very small numbers of this weapon were completed, possibly for delivery to the forces of a country allied to Germany. Whatever the reason, the MP 41 submachine gun seems to have been a complete waste of time, manpower and precious German resources.

SPECIFICATIONS

MP 41

Type:
submachine gun

Calibre:
9mm (0.354in) Parabellum

Length:
0.865m (34in)

Length of barrel:
0.25m (9.9in)

Weight:
3.7kg (8.15lb)

Muzzle velocity:
380m (1247ft) per second

Feed:
32-round detachable magazine (500rpm)

MG 08

SPECIFICATIONS

MG 08

Type:
heavy water-cooled machine gun

Calibre:
7.92mm (0.312in)

Length:
1.175m (46.25in)

Length of barrel:
0.719m (28.3in)

Weight:
62kg (136.7lb) with spares

Muzzle velocity:
900m (2953ft) per second

Feed:
250-round fabric belt (300–450rpm)

The Schwere Maschinengewehr 08 (specification at left) was one of Germany's most important weapons of World War I, and numbers remained in service up to the outbreak of World War II as there were insufficient MG 34 weapons to replace them. By 1942 the s MG 08 had been retired to second-line duties. Captured weapons used by the Germans (with their new designations) included the Belgian 7.65mm Mitrailleuse "Maxim" (7.65mm s MG 221[b]), Lithuanian 7.92mm (7.9mm s MG 248[r]), Polish 7.92mm Maxsim 08 (7.9mm s MG 248[r]) and Yugoslav 7.92mm Mitralez 7.9mm M8M (7.9mm s MG 248[j]). The leichte MG 08/15 was a lightened version of the s MG 08 that kept its predecessor's mechanism and water-cooling, but was fitted with a bipod rather than being installed on a heavy tripod, and had a pistol grip and shoulder stock in place of the s MG 08's pair of spade grips. Turning the scales at a hefty 18kg (39.7lb), the le MG 08/15 was still in first-line service in 1939 but had been retired to second-line use by 1941. Captured weapons used by the Germans included the Belgian 7.65mm Mitrailleuse "Maxim" légère (7.65mm le MG 125[b]), Soviet 7.9mm Rutschnoi pulemet "Maksima" obrazets 08/15 (7.9mm le MG 145[r]), and Yugoslav 7.9mm Leki-Mitralez M8/15M (7.9mm le MG 145[j]).

MG 34

The Maschinengewehr 34 was designed by engineers at the Mauser factory at Obendorff, and major features of this superb machine gun included a quick-change barrel, connection of major components by bayonet catches, high-impact plastic stock, combined recoil booster and flash hider, straight-through design, and a system in which pressure on the upper and lower parts of the trigger produced semi-automatic and automatic fire respectively. In overall terms, therefore, the MG 34 was not so much a light/medium machine gun as the world's first general-purpose machine gun. In the light role the MG 34 was fired off a light bipod, with the Dreifuss 34 tripod mounting used for the anti-aircraft role. In the heavy machine gun role the MG 34 was installed on the Lafette 34 tripod mounting that could also be adapted for the anti-aircraft task. Several other mountings were available to suit the weapon to service in armoured fighting vehicles, wheeled vehicles and fixed fortification, while there were also twin and triple mountings for extra capability in the anti-aircraft task. The MG 34 entered service in 1936 and remained in production and service until 1945. It was an excellent gun, and was especially notable for its accuracy and high rate of fire. The MG 34's one major "failing" was its expense in terms of manufacturing cost and time.

SPECIFICATIONS

MG 34

Type:
general-purpose air-cooled machine gun

Calibre:
7.92mm (0.312in)

Length:
1.219m (48in)

Length of barrel:
0.627m (24.75in)

Weight:
11.5kg (26.7lb) with bipod

Muzzle velocity:
755m (2477ft) per second

Feed:
50-round belt, 50- or 75-round magazine (900rpm)

MG 42

SPECIFICATIONS

MG 42

Type:
general-purpose air-cooled machine gun

Calibre:
7.92mm (0.312in)

Length:
1.22m (48in)

Length of barrel:
0.533m (21in)

Weight:
11.5kg (25lb) with bipod

Muzzle velocity:
755m (2477ft) per second

Feed:
50-round belt, 50- or 75-round magazine (1500rpm)

Without doubt one of the most far-sighted and influential machine guns created in World War II, the Maschinengewehr 42 was in terms of its design and manufacturing requirements a truly outstanding weapon that has exercised a long-lasting influence over later general-purpose machine guns. The Mauser-designed MG 42 began life as the MG 39/41, whose origins could be found in the MG 34 and some Polish thinking. Like the MG 34, the MG 34 could be installed on several alternative mountings, but so far as troops in the field were concerned the MG 42's primary advantage over the MG 34 was its higher rate of fire. The locking system was novel but simple and reliable, the barrel-change system was quick and easy (as demanded by the high rate of fire), and the greatest innovation was the ease with which the weapon could be produced: the use of stampings and spot welding wherever possible to reduce cost and hasten production even when only semi-skilled labour was available. The MG 42 first saw service in North Africa during 1942, and from that time onward the weapon became one of Germany's most important and feared tactical weapons. A final development was the MG 45 with a different mechanism and an even higher rate of fire, but this was only just entering service as the war ended.

REVOLVER NO 2 MK I

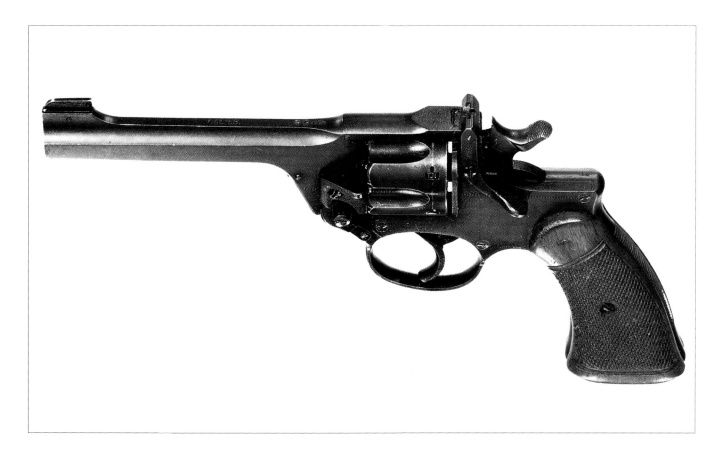

During World War I the British found that while their 0.455in pistol round offered excellent combat capability, the No 1 revolver from which it was fired was too heavy and cumbersome for battlefield use (though the weapon was very accurate). What was needed, the British decided, was a smaller round fired from a lighter pistol that could be handled more easily by men lacking extensive training in the use of heavy pistols. This resulted in the selection of the 0.38in round, for which Webley & Scott created a new pistol that was modified by the Royal Small Arms Factory at Enfield to enter service in 1932 as the Pistol, Revolver, No 2 Mk I. This was a very substantial and well made weapon, but was not deemed wholly satisfactory and was supplanted from 1938 by the No 2 Mk I* pistol with a lighter trigger pull, changed grips and provision for double-action use (requiring the removal of the thumb catch on the hammer).

The No 2 Mk I* was a reliable weapon but was not useful except at close range as the double action made accurate aiming very difficult. From July 1942 the No 2 Mk I** was introduced as a more easily produced model, and one of the changes was the hammer safety stop. The one great advantage with the weapon was its robustness, which meant it could be used in any theatre.

SPECIFICATIONS

REVOLVER NO 2 MK I

Type:
revolver pistol

Calibre:
9.65mm (0.38in)

Length:
0.26m (10.25in)

Length of barrel:
0.127m (5in)

Weight:
0.766kg (1.68lb)

Muzzle velocity:
183m (600ft) per second

Feed:
6-round revolving cylinder

REVOLVER NO 1 MK VI

SPECIFICATIONS

REVOLVER NO 1 MK VI

Type:
revolver pistol

Calibre:
11.56mm (0.455in)

Length:
0.29m (11.25in)

Length of barrel:
0.15m (6in)

Weight:
1.09kg (2.4lb)

Muzzle velocity:
189m (620ft) per second

Feed:
6-round revolving cylinder

The huge 0.455in Webley revolver entered service with the British Army in 1887 after design as a powerful "man stopper" for use mainly in colonial warfare (the British had several disconcerting experiences during their colonial wars, during which native enemies displayed an alarming habit of not dropping to the ground when hit by a round). The final version of this series was introduced in 1915 and became the Pistol, Revolver, .455 No 1 Mk VI.

The other side of the weapon's capability as a potent man-stopper was its weight and general unhandiness, which made it difficult to aim and fire the weapon instinctively at anything but point-blank range. Effective employment of the pistol required considerable training and practice of the types not readily possible in World War I, and this led to the decision to adopt a smaller-calibre revolver, the 9.65mm (0.38in) No 2 weapon. However, at the start of World War II in September 1939 there were large numbers of the 0.455in revolver still in service, and in the UK the type equipped regular units as well as the Home Guard. The Germans felt that the weapon was still useful, for they issued captured revolvers of this type to second-line unit for service with the revised designation Revolver 665(e). As with all Webleys, the design was well made and robust.

RIFLE NO 3 MK I

Teething problems with the Rifle No 1, introduced in 1907, led to consideration of a replacement type firing a 7mm (0.276in) round. The P.13 development model of 1913 was based on a modified Mauser bolt action, but further work of the P.14 definitive model was postponed until 1915, when a variant in 7.7mm (0.303 in) calibre was ordered from American manufacturers for service as the Rifle No 3 Mk I (see specification). The USA later adopted a variant in 7.62mm (0.3in) calibre as the Rifle M1917. The P.14 was long and as a consequence somewhat difficult to handle, but was very accurate and therefore used mainly for sniping. From 1919 the surviving rifles were placed in store, and in 1940 the USA sold more than 750,000 M1917 weapons to the UK, mostly for service with the Home Guard. In 1940, British-made No 3 rifles were converted for sniper use with the designation No 3 Mk I(T), and this saw limited service up to 1943. A variant was the No 3 Mk I(T)A with an Aldis sight. During the interwar period Belgium bought numbers of No 3 rifles, possibly weapons that had been provided to Belgian troops in World War I. FN rebored these guns to 7.92mm calibre, and weapons of this type seized by the Germans after their May 1940 conquest of Belgium were taken into service with the designation Gewehr 284(b).

SPECIFICATIONS

RIFLE NO 3 MK I

Type:
bolt-action rifle

Calibre:
7.7mm (0.303in)

Length:
1.175m (46.25in)

Length of barrel:
0.66m (26in)

Weight:
4.37kg (9.62lb)

Muzzle velocity:
762m (2500ft) per second

Feed:
5-round fixed box magazine

RIFLE NO 4 MK I

SPECIFICATIONS

RIFLE NO 4 MK I

Type:
bolt-action rifle

Calibre:
7.7mm (0.303in)

Length:
1.129m (44.43in)

Length of barrel:
0.64m (25.2in)

Weight:
4.14kg (9.125lb)

Muzzle velocity:
751m (2465ft) per second

Magazine:
10-round detachable box magazine

Work on the design of a rifle to succeed No 1 Mk III* weapon started during 1924. The initial result was the No 1 Mk VI that reached the trials stage and formed the basis of a generally similar rifle optimized for mass production using modern manufacturing techniques. The new weapon was the Rifle No 4 Mk I that first appeared in 1931, although the UK's straitened financial circumstances of the period meant that full-scale manufacture did not start until 1940.

Although a primary consideration in its design had been ease of production, the No 4 Mk I was in no way an indifferent weapon as it was more accurate than earlier models as a result of its heavier barrel and longer sight base. However, the rifle was rushed into production during 1940 and this led to the emergence of several teething problems when the new weapon entered full-scale service in the following year.

A revision of assembly practices cured these difficulties, and the No 4 rifle then streamed off the production lines in vast numbers. The No 4 Mk I*, with only slight differences, was placed in production in Canada and the USA, and the weapon was also made in India. Another variant, the No 4 Mk I(T), was a sniping model with a telescopic sight and a cheek stock. This rifle was a very robust weapon.

STEN GUN

One of the weapons which the British Army needed most urgently as it sought to re-equip after its expulsion from mainland Europe in June 1940 was a submachine gun that was cheap and easy to manufacture. At the Royal Small Arms Factory at Enfield Lock R.V. Shepperd and H.J. Turpin created a very simple weapon that was accepted as the Sten.

Cheapness and ease of manufacture drove the basic design, and the Sten Mk I entered service in the summer of 1941. The Mk I had a flash hider and a wooden forestock and grip, but the Mk I* lacked these. Then came the Mk II (the specifications for which are given in the table at right) that was an even simpler weapon: the barrel, for example, was a drawn steel tube with only two rifling grooves, although these were later increased in number to six. Fairly reliable and very simple to maintain, the Sten was also easy to conceal and was much favoured by resistance forces. Germany used captured weapons with the designation Maschinenpistole 749(e) and produced copies as the MP 3008. The Mk II(S) was also a silenced version of the Mk II, the Mk III was a simplified version of the Mk I, the Mk IV was an experimental model for airborne forces, the Mk V was a less austere version of the Mk III, and the Mk VI was a silenced Mk V.

SPECIFICATIONS

STEN GUN

Type:
submachine gun

Calibre:
9mm (0.354in) Parabellum

Length:
0.762m (30in)

Length of barrel:
0.197m (7.75in)

Weight:
3kg (6.625lb)

Muzzle velocity:
366m (1200ft) per second

Feed:
32-round detachable box magazine (540rpm)

BREN GUN

SPECIFICATIONS

BREN GUN

Type:
light air-cooled machine gun

Calibre:
7.7mm (0.303in)

Length:
1.155m (45.5in)

Length of barrel:
0.635m (25in)

Weight:
9.95kg (22.12lb)

Muzzle velocity:
744m (2440ft) per second

Feed:
30-round detachable curved box magazine (500rpm)

The Bren Gun, one of the most famous light machine guns of World War II, had its origins in a Czechoslovak weapon, the ZB vz/26, via the vz/27, vz/30, vz/33 and vz/34. This superb gas-operated light machine gun entered production during 1937, its name reflecting its design origins in Brno and manufacture at Enfield Lock. There were four main models in World War II. The Mk I (specification at left) featured an adjustable bipod, butt handle and a rear sight of the radial type, gradually replaced in the Mk II by simpler and cheaper elements as wartime exigencies started to bite. The closely related Mks III and IV were both introduced in 1944 with a shorter and lighter barrel and, in the case of the Mk IV, changes to the butt.

The Bren Gun was at first made only at Enfield Lock, but production then spread to Australia, Canada and India. The Bren Gun was widely used by resistance forces in Europe, a task in which the weapon's light weight, accuracy, good firepower, reliability and ease of maintenance were invaluable. The Germans used captured weapons with the designation 7.7mm leichte Maschinengewehr 138(e). In British use the weapon was mounted on many different types of vehicle mounting and several tripod mountings were developed to complement the standard bipod.

VICKERS-BERTHIER

During 1925 Vickers obtained rights to the Berthier light machine gun, beginning manufacture of the Vickers-Berthier with weapons for export and British trials. The British Army preferred the Bren Gun, but the Indian Army secured large numbers for use as its standard light machine gun. The Mks I and II came from the UK, but then Indian production produced the Mks III (specification at right) and IIIB. The Vickers-Berthier light machine gun was reliable, but scored only limited sales success in markets such as Latvia, Lithuania, Spain and some South American countries. The weapons of the two Baltic states were taken over by the Soviet Union, after its 1939 annexation of these nations, for second-line service with the designation Rutschnoi pulemet "Vickers-Berthier".

Another development of the Vickers-Berthier machine gun was the Vickers G.O. (Gas Operated) or "K" gun with a 96-round drum magazine, which was used mainly as a trainable aeroplane gun until replaced by the Browning gun. Weapons made surplus to Royal Air Force requirement by this process found a second life in airfield defence or on vehicles employed in the North African campaign of 1940–43, especially those of units such as the Long-Range Desert Group and the Special Air Service.

SPECIFICATIONS

VICKERS-BERTHIER

Type:
light air-cooled machine gun

Calibre:
7.7mm (0.303in)

Length:
1.156m (45.5in)

Length of barrel:
0.60m (23.6in)

Weight:
10.9kg (24.4lb)

Muzzle velocity:
747m (2450ft) per second

Feed:
30-round round curved box magazine (450–600rpm)

VICKERS .303 MK I

SPECIFICATIONS

VICKERS .303 MK I

Type:
heavy water-cooled machine gun

Calibre:
7.7mm (0.303in)

Length:
1.156m (45.5in)

Length of barrel:
0.721m (28.4in)

Weight:
18.1kg (40lb) for the gun with cooling water

Muzzle velocity:
744m (2440ft) per second

Feed:
250-round fabric belt (450–500rpm)

The Vickers Machine Gun Mk I entered service in 1912 and throughout its long production life remained essentially unaltered. The weapon was based on the Maxim gas-operated mechanism in an inverted form, and detail changes were introduced to create an extremely sturdy and reliable weapon that served the British and Commonwealth armies with great success in World Wars I and II. The weapon also achieved considerable export success to nations such as Latvia, Lithuania, the Netherlands, Russia and the USA. A few small changes were introduced over the weapon's production life, these variations including a smooth rather than corrugated water jacket, and differences in the muzzle recoil booster. Another mid-life change came with the introduction of the Mk 7z or Mk 8z nitrocellulose-loaded ammunition, which added another 915m (1000 yards) of range to the figure of 3290m (3600 yards) achieved with the original Mk 7 cordite-loaded ammunition, and suggested the adoption in 1942 of an optional dial sight for indirect fire. In World War I the US Army adopted the Vickers gun in 7.62mm (0.3in) calibre as the M1915, and in 1940 the 7000 or so surviving guns were sold back to the UK. The Germans designated captured British, Dutch and Soviet guns 7.7mm s MG 230(e), Dutch 7.7mm s MG 231(h) and 7.7mm s MG 230(r), respectively.

LEWIS GUN

The Lewis light machine gun was created by an American, Samuel McClean, but developed and marketed by another American, Colonel Isaac Lewis, and then first placed in production in Belgium and the UK prior to World War I before finally entering US manufacture during that war.

The Lewis gun was developed as an infantry weapon with a forced-draft cooling system, but was also used in aircraft with the barrel jacket removed as the slipstream served to cool the weapon. Between the two world wars the Lewis gun was produced in Belgium, France, Japan, the UK and the USA, and was widely exported. On the outbreak of World War II in 1939 the Lewis gun was still in very widespread service, and saw extensive use as the armament of merchant ships, for the defence of fixed land installations in single, double and quadruple mountings, and on the vehicles of special forces units, especially in North Africa.

The Germans used captured weapons including (German designation in parentheses) the British 7.7mm Lewis Gun Mk I (7.7mm le MG 137[e]), Dutch 6.5mm Mitrailleur M20 (6.5mm le MG 100[h]) and Soviet 7.62mm Rutschnoi pulemet "Lewis" (7.62mm le MG 122[r]). The Lewis was an excellent weapon, being both reliable and robust.

SPECIFICATIONS

LEWIS GUN

Type:
light air-cooled machine gun

Calibre:
7.7mm (0.303in)

Length:
1.25m (49.2in)

Length of barrel:
0.661m (26.04in)

Weight:
12.15kg (27lb)

Muzzle velocity:
744m (2440ft) per second

Feed:
47- or 97-round overhead drum magazine (450rpm)

PISTOLA M1889

SPECIFICATIONS

PISTOLA M1889

Type:
revolver pistol

Calibre:
10.35mm (0.4075in)

Length:
0.23m (9.07in)

Length of barrel:
0.122m (4.79in)

Weight:
0.91kg (2lb)

Muzzle velocity:
255m (837ft) per second

Feed:
6-round revolving cylinder

There can be little doubt that the Pistola a Rotazione modello 1889 must have been in concept, if not necessarily in manufacture, one of the oldest types of pistol still in service in June 1940, when Italy entered World War II as one of the Axis powers. Although the weapon was introduced to Italian service in 1889, it was in fact derived from a revolver first issued to the Italian army in 1872. The modello 1889 was a sturdy and reliable rather than inspired revolver, and was retained in production right into the 1920s: there was no single source for the type, although the largest number was produced by Glisenti, so there were a number of detail differences between the revolvers manufactured by different companies.

It is possible that there were some 60 variations, large and small, and the most evident of these was in the region of the trigger. Here the modello 1889 could be found with a folding trigger and no trigger guard, or alternatively with a fixed trigger and trigger guard. Other elements in which they were variations were in the materials, the shaping of the hammer, the shaping of the butt, and the precise nature of the safety system used. Despite its obsolete nature, the modello 1889 was widely used by the Italian Army in every theatre in which Italian forces were involved.

BERETTA M1934

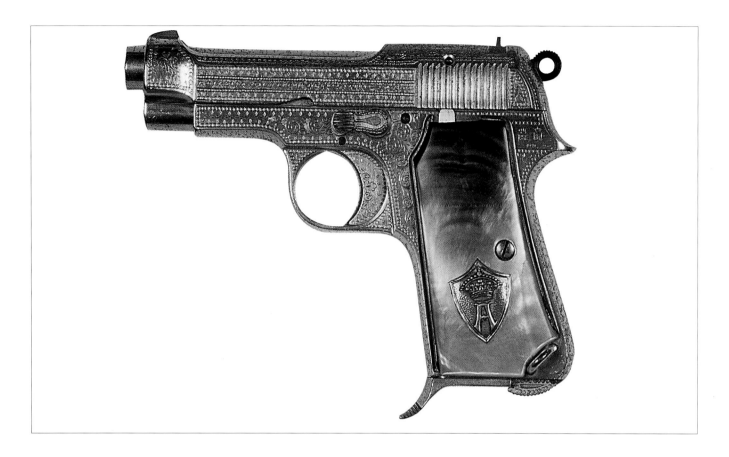

The first semi-automatic pistol by the celebrated Pietro Beretta SpA company of Italy was the modello 1915, which entered service with the Italian Army in the year in which Italy entered World War I as one of the Allied powers. This pioneering weapon was succeeded by the modello 1922 in 7.65mm calibre, the modello 1923 that was the first Beretta semi-automatic pistol with an external hammer and fired a 9mm round of the low-powered Glisenti type, and then the modello 1931 in 7.65mm calibre with a straighter grip and intended for use mainly by the Italian Navy.

These paved the way to the Pistola Automatica Beretta modello 1934 (specification at right), which was taken into large-scale service as the Italian Army's standard semi-automatic pistol of World War II. This gun was generally manufactured in 9mm calibre, the round being of the 9mm modello 1934 *corto* (short) type, but small numbers were completed in 7.65mm calibre. The modello 1934 was invariably finished to a very high standard, and after their seizure of northern Italy after September 1943 the Germans took into service all the weapons they could with the revised designation 9mm Pistole 671(i). A smaller and lighter version of the modello 1934 was produced as the 7.65mm modello 35 for the Italian Air Force.

SPECIFICATIONS

BERETTA M1934

Type:
semi-automatic pistol

Calibre:
9mm (0.354in) modello 1934 corto

Length:
0.152m (6in)

Length of barrel:
0.0865m (3.4in)

Weight:
0.617kg (1.36lb)

Muzzle velocity:
245m (804ft) per second

Feed:
7-round detachable straight box magazine

FUCILE M91

SPECIFICATIONS

FUCILE M91

Type:
bolt-action rifle

Calibre:
6.5mm (0.256in)

Length:
1.285m (50.6in)

Length of barrel:
0.78m (30.7in)

Weight:
3.8kg (8.4lb)

Muzzle velocity:
630m (2,067ft) per second

Feed:
6-rounded fixed box magazine

The Fucile modello 91 was the first rifle of the Mauser-Paravicino or Mannlicher-Carcano type (Mauser one-piece bolt with front locking lugs and Mannlicher integral magazine loaded by means of a six-round clip that remained in the magazine until the last round was chambered) to be taken into service with the Italian Army. This took place in 1892, and the bolt action was that of the Mauser Gewehr 1889 modified with a Carcano bolt-sleeve safety mechanism, while Paravicino was the name of the general heading the commission that selected the weapon.

The modello 91 was the Italian Army's standard rifle right throughout the whole of World War I, and was still in large-scale service when Italy entered World War II in June 1940, when Mussolini invaded France. The Germans seized numbers of these rifles from September 1943 to equip elements for their forces in Italy, the revised designation being Gewehr 214(i), and in 1944 rebored small numbers to take the German standard 7.92mm round. Yugoslavia had also bought the modello 91 for service as the Puska 6.5mm M91, and the Germans used captured examples with the designation Gewehr 214(j). In 1905, Japan secured limited numbers of a modello 91 in a Rifle Type I variant chambered for the Japanese 6.5mm round.

FUCILE M38

The Fucile modello 38 has the distinction of being the first rifle created for a new Italian 7.35mm cartridge. The rifle was in fact a straightforward development of the 6.5mm modello 91 weapon with a larger-calibre barrel and modified sights. The weapon entered service in 1938, but the Italian authorities realized at this point that Italy's entry into a general European war could no longer be delayed.

Given the availability of vast quantities of 6.5mm ammunition already available, the decision was then made to revise the modello 38 to fire the older type of cartridge: most (but not all) of the existing rifles were fitted with a new barrel, and new-production weapons were produced in the smaller calibre. The inevitable result was a logistic nightmare that was still affecting the Italian Army up to the time of Italy's September 1943 armistice with the Allies.

Following Italy's exit from the war, the Germans took over stocks of the weapons for use with the designations 6.5mm Gewehr 209(i) and 7.35mm Gewehr 231(i). The Germans also tried to resolve the calibre problem by reboring weapons to 7.92mm calibre, but the power of the German cartridge meant that the resulting weapon was not safe. There was also a carbine version known as the Moschetto modello 1938 per cavalleria.

SPECIFICATIONS

FUCILE M38

Type:
bolt-action rifle

Calibre:
6.5 and 7.35mm (0.256 and 0.289in)

Length:
1.02m (40.2in)

Length of barrel:
0.54m (21.1in)

Weight:
3.45kg (7.6lb)

Muzzle velocity:
707m (2320ft) per second

Feed:
6-round fixed straight box magazine

BERETTA M1918

SPECIFICATIONS

BERETTA M1918

Type:
submachine gun

Calibre:
9mm (0.354in) Glisenti

Length:
0.85m (33.5in)

Length of barrel:
0.317m (12.5in)

Weight:
3.27kg (7.2lb)

Muzzle velocity:
390m (1280ft) per second

Feed:
25-round detachable box magazine (900rpm)

The world's first submachine gun, entering service in 1915, was the Villar Perosa that comprised a pair of weapons mounted on a vehicle pintle or shoulder-supported tray and controlled by means of spade grips to the sides of the thumb trigger mechanism. After World War I the Villar Perosa was developed for shoulder-fired use as the Officine Villar Perosa single-barrel weapon with a wooden stock and a conventional trigger. However, before the end of the war Tullio Marengoni of the Beretta company of Brescia in northern Italy had already created a more practical weapon, based on the same type of retarded blowback mechanism as the Villar Perosa and firing the same 9mm Glisenti low-powered round, as the Moschetto Automatico Beretta modello 1918 (see specification). The modello 1918 had a full set of wooden furniture, a completely new trigger arrangement, a modified operating mechanism to slow the rate of fire, and even a folding bayonet. The modello 1918 was also manufactured in two variants, one of them with a pair of triggers (for automatic and single-shot fire) and one with a single trigger for semi-automatic fire only. The modello 1918 drew its ammunition from an overhead magazine, but the modello 1918/30 was a revision firing the higher-powered 9mm Parabellum round from a magazine shifted through 180° to a position directly under the weapon.

BERETTA M38

Designed by Tullio Marengoni of the Beretta company and accepted for service in 1938, the Moschetto Automatico modello 38A was one of the company's most successful products. The weapon had good performance and was also very reliable as a result of its good design and the excellence with which it was manufactured. The first weapons of this type were chambered for a special round, the 9mm *cartucchia pallottola modello* 38A, but the demands of a growing number of export customers, especially in South America, for a variant using the more readily available 9mm Parabellum round meant that later weapons were chambered for this cartridge.

The type was also sold to Romania, and Germany used the weapon from 1941 with the designation 9mm Maschinenpistole 739(i). The modello 38A had four primary subvariants, none of them dignified by a particular designation. The first had provision for a bayonet and featured a compensator on the muzzle; the second had a barrel jacket in which the original slots were replaced by circular holes; the third appeared late in 1938 without provision for a bayonet and featuring a four-slot compensator; and the fourth appeared late in 1940 as a more easily produced type with a barrel jacket welded from stampings.

SPECIFICATIONS

BERETTA M38

Type:
submachine gun

Calibre:
9mm (0.354in)

Length:
0.947m (37.3in)

Length of barrel:
0.32m (12.6in)

Weight:
3.945kg (8.7lb)

Muzzle velocity:
450m (1476ft) per second

Feed:
10-, 20- or 40-round box magazine (550–600rpm)

BERETTA M38/42

SPECIFICATIONS

BERETTA M38/42

Type:
submachine gun

Calibre:
9mm (0.354in) Parabellum

Length:
0.80m (31.5in)

Length of barrel:
0.20m (7.87in)

Weight:
3.27kg (7.2lb)

Muzzle velocity:
450m (1476ft) per second

Feed:
20- or 40-round detachable box magazine (550rpm)

In service the Beretta modello 38A submachine gun revealed itself to be a first-class weapon of its type, but it also became abundantly clear that the modello 38A was not suited in production and cost terms to large-scale manufacture under the increasingly austere conditions imposed on Italy by World War II. Beretta therefore undertook the task of simplifying the modello 38A into a weapon that offered basically unaltered operational capabilities but was easier and therefore cheaper to make. The result was the Moschetto Automatico Beretta modello 38/42 (see specification at left). This made use of stamped steel components wherever possible, had no barrel jacket, fired 9mm ammunition of the Parabellum rather than lower-powered Glisenti type, and was provided with a new form of dust-protected bolt to improve reliability under adverse conditions such as those found in the North African campaign and the Italian sector of the Eastern Front. Even so, the modello 38/42 still emerged as a weapon of notably high quality that was used by the Italians, Romanians and Germans, the last of whom issued the 9mm Maschinenpistole 738(i) to their forces in Italy and North Africa. The modelli 38/43 and 38/44 were later variants with further changes to speed and cheapen manufacture still further.

FIAT M14

Italy's standard machine gun of World War I was the 6.5mm Revelli modello 1914 manufactured mostly by Fiat and often known as the Fiat-Revelli. From 1935 significant numbers of these obsolescent weapons were improved to Mitriaglice Fiat modello 1914/35 standard, with guns built to the same standard receiving the designation modello 35. The primary alteration was effected in the feed system, in which the original Revelli type of 50-round magazine divided into 10 five-round compartments was replaced by a belt feed, but another major change was the replacement of the original water-cooled barrel by a heavier air-cooled barrel of the quick-change type in the new Italian calibre of 8mm. It was hoped that the changes (including a fluted chamber) would remove the need for the cartridge-oiling system used in the modello 14 to facilitate the extraction of spent cartridges, but this cumbersome and dirt-attracting system had in fact to be retained.

The modello 1914/35 was actually a worse gun than the modello 1914, one of its poorest features being the tendency of the barrel to overheat very rapidly. Even so, the modello 1914/35 was retained through World War II for lack of an adequate replacement, and the Germans used small numbers of this poor weapon with the designation 8mm s MG 255(i).

SPECIFICATIONS

FIAT M14

Type:
medium air-cooled machine gun

Calibre:
8mm (0.315in)

Length:
1.2635m (49.75in)

Length of barrel:
0.654m (25.75in)

Weight:
17.9kg (39.75lb) gun; 18.7kg (41.5lb) for the tripod

Muzzle velocity:
790m (2592ft) per second

Feed:
300-round non-disintegrating belt (500rpm)

BREDA M30

SPECIFICATIONS

BREDA M30

Type:
light air-cooled machine gun

Calibre:
6.5mm (0.256in)

Length:
1.232m (48.5in)

Length of barrel:
0.520m (20.5in)

Weight:
10.24kg (22.75lb)

Muzzle velocity:
630m (2067ft) per second

Feed:
20-round fixed straight box magazine (450–500rpm)

The 6.5mm Fucile Mitriagliatori Breda modello 30 was a light machine gun evolved via the modello 1924, modello 1928 and modello 1929 weapons of the same type, and served through Italy's involvement in World War II as the Italian Army's standard light machine gun. In many respects the modello 1930 was a distinctly poor weapon, but for lack of any viable alternative it was retained in service and saw extensive use, especially in the see-saw campaign waged in North Africa. Like the Revelli modello 1914, the modello 1930 was of the delayed blowback type with a recoiling barrel and a massive bolt carrying several locking lugs, and this demanded the use of an oiling mechanism to lubricate the cartridge cases, before they were loaded, so that adequate extraction of spent cases could be achieved: the oiler attracted significant quantities of dirt and dust, especially under North African conditions, and this was the cause of repeated jammings. Two other poor features of the design were the magazine and quick-change barrel. The magazine was permanently attached to the right-hand side of the weapon by a hinge that allowed the unit to be swung forward for loading: any damage or distortion of this magazine rendered the modello 1930 inoperative. The barrel lacked a handle, which meant that barrel changing was singularly slow.

BREDA M37

Created as the successor to the modello 1914/35, the Mitriaglice Breda modello 37 (see specification) emerged in World War II as the best Italian heavy machine gun for land-based service. A significant improvement was effected over the earlier weapon in the use of gas rather than delayed blowback operation, but a system to oil the cartridges was still employed and the feed system was decidedly odd as rounds were fed into the gun from a 20-round flat tray into which the spent cases were then returned: this meant that the spent cases then had to be dumped before the magazine could be reloaded. Even so, the modello 37 proved itself a sturdy and reliable weapon, qualities that endeared it to the troops in the field, especially those fighting in the heat of North Africa or on the freezing steppes of Russia, and the type could be installed on a tall tripod mounting for use in the anti-aircraft role.

The Germans operated limited numbers of modello 37 machine guns with the designation 8mm s MG 259(i). The modello 37 was also developed into a variant for use in armoured fighting vehicles. Entering service in 1938, this Mitriaglice Breda calibro 8 modello 38 per carri armati (known to the Germans as the 8mm Kpfw MG 350[i]) had a conventional curved box magazine above the weapon, and was generally mounted on assault guns.

SPECIFICATIONS

BREDA M37

Type:
heavy air-cooled machine gun

Calibre:
8mm (0.315in)

Length:
1.27m (50in)

Length of barrel:
0.74m (29.1in)

Weight:
19.3kg (42.8lb) gun; 18.7kg (41.5lb) tripod mounting

Muzzle velocity:
790m (2592ft) per second

Feed:
20-round strip (450rpm)

PISTOL TYPE 26

SPECIFICATIONS

PISTOL TYPE 26

Type:
  revolver pistol

Calibre:
  9mm (0.354in)

Length:
  0.24m (9.4in)

Length of barrel:
  0.12m (4.7in)

Weight:
  0.9kg (2lb)

Muzzle velocity:
  275m (902ft) per second

Feed:
  6-round cylinder

The Revolver Pistol Type 26 weapon entered service, initially with cavalry units of the Imperial Japanese Army, in the course of 1893. The design of this revolver blended a number of American and European design features, including break-open access to the cylinder typical of the American Smith & Wesson company and lock work derived from that of the Austro-Hungarian Rast and Gasser.

The revolver had two notably unusual features in being double-action only (in the fashion of later British-designed 0.38in/9.65mm Enfield revolvers) and chambered for a unique 9mm rimmed pistol round. One good feature of the design was its hinged side plate, which provided easy access to the lock work. From 1925 this indifferent revolver was replaced as the Japanese Army's standard pistol by a semi-automatic weapon, but despite this fact remained in large-scale service and was widely used in World War II. Like many revolvers of its type, this weapon was very sturdy, and could operate in inhospitable terrain. In addition – and this was very important to Japanese troops operating in the Pacific on islands that were often far from workshops – it was easy to maintain: it could be stripped and re-assembled very quickly (it had relatively few working parts).

PISTOL TYPE 14

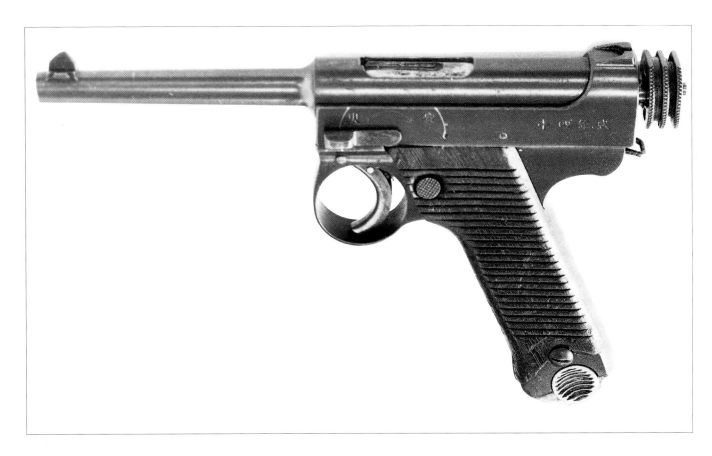

Introduced in 1925, the Pistol Type 14 pistol was designed by Colonel Kijiro Nambu and manufactured by the Kayoba Factory Co. Ltd. as the specifically military version of Nambu's 8mm Pistol Type 1904. The 1904 model had been created for the commercial market, but even so had secured major sales to Japanese officers wanting a pistol more advanced than the Type 26 revolver (see page opposite).

By comparison with the Type 1904, the Type 14 had a manual rather than grip safety, a magazine with a safety, and a rear sight of the fixed notch rather than tangent type and, as a more obvious external difference, a narrower butt. The mechanism was also modified slightly, and the weapon's construction was beefed-up for service use. These modifications could not conceal the fact, however, that the Type 14 was still an indifferent pistol that was altogether too prone to reliability problems. The Type 14 (Modified), which was introduced in 1938, was fitted with a larger trigger guard to allow the weapon's use by men wearing gloves. More modern designs, of course, usually meant more working parts and more intricate working mechanisms. These were fine on ranges and on the parade ground, but in the mud and grime of battle they were found wanting – with often fatal results for the user.

SPECIFICATIONS

PISTOL TYPE 14

Type:
semi-automatic pistol

Calibre:
8mm (0.315in)

Length:
0.23m (9in)

Length of barrel:
0.12m (4.75in)

Weight:
0.91kg (2lb)

Muzzle velocity:
325m (1066ft) per second

Feed:
8-round detachable straight box magazine

PISTOL TYPE 94

SPECIFICATIONS

PISTOL TYPE 94

Type:
  semi-automatic pistol

Calibre:
  8mm (0.315in)

Length:
  0.183m (7.2in)

Length of barrel:
  0.096m (3.8in)

Weight:
  0.766kg (1.69lb)

Muzzle velocity:
  325m (1066ft) per second

Feed:
  6-round detachable straight box magazine

Arguably one of the worst if not actually the worst semi-automatic pistol ever placed in full military service, the Type 94 pistol was introduced in 1934 and, securing virtually no civil sales, was manufactured in the Japanese Army's own arsenals as the side arm of the Imperial Japanese Army's officers. Service use very rapidly revealed the extent of the weapon's deficiencies, which included an acute lack of "pointability", a sear that was exposed on the left-hand side of the receiver in a fashion that allowed it to be jolted and so discharge the weapon, and a locking mechanism that allowed the weapon to be fired without the receiver being locked, especially if poor maintenance had allowed the relevant parts to be worn down.

All these factors were bad enough when the pistol was manufactured under peace-time conditions, but the situation became worse still after Japan's December 1941 entry into World War II resulted in a steady degradation of quality control to the extent that late-production examples of the Type 14 were as dangerous to the firer as the target it was being aimed at! Work on the design of a replacement pistol was launched in 1942 and resulted in the Type 11 pistol, but progress was slow and only some 500 of these guns had been completed before Japan's defeat in 1945.

RIFLE TYPE 38

The Rifle Type 38 was an evolutionary development of the Rifle Type 30 designed by Colonel Arisaka, and was thus often known by the Japanese as the Arisaka Rifle. The Type 30 (and thus the Type 38) was based on the Mauser bolt action as exemplified in the Gewehr 98 but modified in elements of its cocking (during the forward movement of the bolt as on the Lee Enfield) and its safety (the Mauser type of flag-type safety being replaced by a knob on the rear of the bolt that was pushed in and turned to lock the firing pin).

The Type 38 fired a relatively low-powered cartridge, and in combination with a long barrel this resulted in low recoil forces, which was a factor that suited the generally small size and light weight of the average Japanese infantryman. However, the length of the rifle made the Type 38 a weapon difficult to handle, especially after the long Type 30 bayonet had been fitted, which the Japanese always favoured.

The Type 38 was the standard Japanese Army rifle in the period after the end of the Russo-Japanese War in 1905, and remained in service right through to the end of World War II. The weapon was also exported to Siam (later Thailand). Adopted in 1937, the Type 97 was a sniper version of the Type 38. Overall it was a reliable and robust weapon.

SPECIFICATIONS

RIFLE TYPE 38

Type:
bolt-action rifle

Calibre:
6.5mm (0.256in)

Length:
1.275m (50.2in)

Length of barrel:
0.7975m (31.4in)

Weight:
4.2kg (9.25lb)

Muzzle velocity:
730m (2395ft) per second

Feed:
5-round fixed box magazine

CARBINE TYPE 38

SPECIFICATIONS

CARBINE TYPE 38

Type:
bolt-action carbine

Calibre:
6.5mm (0.256in)

Length:
0.869m (34.2in)

Length of barrel:
0.506m (19.9in)

Weight:
3.3kg (7.3lb)

Muzzle velocity:
700m (2297ft) per second

Feed:
5-round fixed box magazine

An exact contemporary of the Rifle Type 38, being introduced to service in 1905, the Carbine Type 38 was basically similar to the rifle and differed significantly only in the length of its barrel. The weapon was intended for service with mounted troops, but with the decline of this branch of the Imperial Japanese Army during the 1930s the Carbine Type 38 was by 1941 the weapon mainly of second-line forces and also with the garrisons of fixed installations, including fortress areas. Like the Rifle Type 38, the Carbine Type 38 was also captured in large enough numbers by the Chinese to equip several formations. It is curious that this weapon was not adopted in greater numbers by Japanese frontline formations, as its performance was only marginally less than the longer Type 38. No doubt the psychological effect that the longer rifles with bayonets attached had on the enemy had something to do with the choice of weapon.

The shorter length and lower weight of the Carbine Type 38 by comparison with the Rifle Type 38 also commended the Carbine Type 38 as the basis for the personal weapon of the Japanese airborne forces, which received limited numbers of a version with a butt that was hinged to fold to the right as a means of reducing length still further.

RIFLE TYPE 99

From 1932 Japanese forces gradually adopted a heavier 7.7mm cartridge for use in the Type 92 machine gun, and in 1939 a rimless derivative of this cartridge was introduced, despite the fact that the higher recoil forces were difficult for the average Japanese soldier to handle, as the ammunition for an improved Rifle Type 99 version of the Type 38 rifle. The opportunity was taken to introduce a number of other changes, these including a rear sight designed to provide anti-aircraft capability through the addition of folding lateral arms marked off for speed "lead", a folding wire monopod, and alterations designed to ease production.

As the effects of World War II on Japanese war industries became more acute, further changes were introduced (including a conventional rear sight) to simplify production with poorer materials and less skilled manpower, and from 1943 the weapon was decidedly crude in manufacture and finish. There were two models which differed only in barrel length (the specification applies to the shorter-barrel model), and another model was made for airborne troops. This last model could be broken into two sections (connected by a spring-loaded plunger) by means of an interrupted thread in the barrel just forward of the receiver, and had a bolt handle that could be removed.

SPECIFICATIONS

RIFLE TYPE 99

Type:
bolt-action rifle

Calibre:
7.7mm (0.303in)

Length:
1.275m (50.1in)

Length of barrel:
0.655m (25.8in)

Weight:
3.9kg (8.6lb)

Muzzle velocity:
730m (2395ft) per second

Feed:
5-round fixed box magazine

SMG TYPE 100

SPECIFICATIONS

SMG TYPE 100

Type:
submachine gun

Calibre:
8mm (0.315in)

Length:
0.867m (34in) butt extended; 0.564m (22.2in) folded

Length of barrel:
0.228m (9in)

Weight:
3.83kg (8.5lb)

Muzzle velocity:
335m (1099ft) per second

Feed:
30-round detachable box magazine (450rpm)

Japan was initially less enthusiastic about the capabilities of the submachine gun than the armies of the Western world, and up to the late 1930s the Imperial Japanese Army was content to import Bergmann Model 1920 weapons from Switzerland in limited numbers for evaluation and the equipment of some small special forces units. In 1940, however, the Japanese introduced their first submachine gun of indigenous design, the Sub-Machine Gun Type 100 created by the army's own ordnance branch under the supervision of General Kijiro Nambu. The Type 100 was manufactured in three forms, one with a fixed butt, a bayonet lug bar and sometimes a compensator, one with a folding butt and bayonet lug bar (see specification) for airborne forces, and one delivered from 1944 as a simplified weapon with a fixed butt, a bayonet lug on the barrel jacket, a compensator and a fixed-aperture rear sight.

All three variants of the Type 100 fired the Japanese 8mm pistol round, and were capable of automatic fire only. The design could be regarded most charitably as indifferent, and the service use of the weapon was bedevilled by the poor quality of the ammunition. Production amounted to perhaps 10,000 and 7500 examples of the fixed- and folding-butt variants respectively.

HMG TYPE 3

Impressed with the capabilities of the Hotchkiss modèle 1900 heavy machine gun, of which it had used small numbers in the Russo-Japanese War of 1904–05, the Imperial Japanese Army decided to order a locally developed version optimized for Japanese manufacturing techniques. The result was the Heavy Machine Gun Type 3 that was adopted in 1914 as a development of the baseline French weapon with the calibre altered from 8mm to 6.5mm and the modifications effected in the ejector system.

The Type 3 was the standard heavy machine gun of the Japanese Army for many years, and in overall configuration was very similar to the French original except in features such as fittings at the base of the tripod legs for the insertion of carrying poles, more cooling fins on the barrel, and an oiling mechanism to lubricate the cartridges as they were fed into the gun from the Hotchkiss type of ammunition strip.

The Japanese forces still had large numbers of the Type 3 machine gun in their inventories in 1941, and though forces in the field appreciated the weapon's basic soundness and reliability, they were less favourably disposed to its poor range and low stopping power with the 6.5mm round, as well as the inadequate 30-round ammunition strips it fired.

SPECIFICATIONS

HMG TYPE 3

Type:
heavy air-cooled machine gun

Calibre:
6.5mm (0.256in)

Length:
1.37m (45.5in)

Length of barrel:
0.745m (29.2in)

Weight:
28.1kg (62lb) gun; 27.2kg (60lb) tripod mounting

Muzzle velocity:
745m (2444ft) per second

Feed:
30-round metal strips (400–500rpm)

LMG TYPE 11

SPECIFICATIONS

LMG TYPE 11

Type:
light air-cooled machine gun

Calibre:
6.5mm (0.256in)

Length:
1.105m (43.5in)

Length of barrel:
0.483m (19in)

Weight:
10.1kg (22.5lb)

Muzzle velocity:
700m (2297ft) per second

Feed:
30-round hopper using six 5-round clips (500rpm)

The Light Machine Gun Type 11 entered service with the Imperial Japanese Army in the course of 1922 and its design, though modelled on Hotchkiss thinking, was unusual in many ways. The weapon was designed by General Kijiro Nambu and was still the infantry's standard light machine gun when Japan entered World War II in December 1941. The weapon remained in service throughout Japan's involvement in World War II even though superior machine guns were created to replace it.

The Type 11 machine gun had an unusual feed arrangement in the form of a hopper filled with a stack of standard rifle ammunition clips as used by Japanese infantrymen: the concept was sound, but in practice the mechanism was too complex for effective field use and therefore presented problems that could be solved only by the introduction of a lower-powered round, resulting in generally reduced overall performance.

Despite its numerous shortcomings, the Type 11 light machine gun saw very extensive service. The weapon possessed a very distinctive butt attached to the rear of the trigger guard and the underside of the receiver, and could be fired from either in inbuilt bipod (as shown in the above photograph) or, for the sustained-fire role, a tripod mounting.

LMG TYPE 96

Entering service in 1936, the Light Machine Gun Type 96 was conceived and developed as the successor to the indifferent and obsolescent Light Machine Gun Type 11, but Japanese production under wartime conditions was so slow that the new weapon in fact supplemented rather than supplanted the older machine gun. The Type 96 was of modern concept by the standards of the day, and combined features which the Japanese design team copied from the French Hotchkiss and Czechoslovak ZB vz.26 weapon.

One of the most important conceptual changes in the Type 96 was the replacement of the Type 11's hopper feed system with an overhead box magazine of the Czechoslovak type, but even though the reduced-power Type 30 cartridge was used, the Type 96 had to keep the Type 11's type of cartridge-lubrication system with all its dirt-catching propensities. Two good features were the introduction of a quick-change barrel capability, and the facility to use either drum or telescopic sights. Another feature, and one perhaps unique among service machine guns, was the provision for a bayonet. This was a peculiar Japanese trait, and was totally useless as the task of machine guns was to support charging infantrymen as they made their bayonet attacks, rather than running alongside them.

SPECIFICATIONS

LMG TYPE 96

Type:
light air-cooled machine gun

Calibre:
6.5mm (0.256in)

Length:
1.055m (41.5in)

Barrel length:
0.55m (21.65in)

Weight:
9.07kg (20lb)

Muzzle velocity:
730m (2395ft) per second

Feed:
30-round detachable curved magazine (550rpm)

HMG TYPE 92

SPECIFICATIONS

HMG TYPE 92

Type:
  heavy air-cooled machine gun

Calibre:
  7.7mm (0.303in)

Length:
  1.156m (45.5in)

Length of barrel:
  0.749mm (29.5in)

Weight:
  55.3kg (122lb) with tripod mounting

Muzzle velocity:
  730m (2395ft) per second

Feed:
  30-round metal strip (450–500rpm)

The tactical limitations of the relatively low-powered 6.5mm rifle cartridge were appreciated by the Japanese during and after World War I, and in 1932 the Japanese ammunition development service pioneered a more powerful 7.7mm round offering longer range and greater hitting power throughout its range bracket.

Of the new weapons produced to exploit the capabilities of the new round, one of the first was the Heavy Machine Gun Type 92 that was standardized in 1932. This was in effect a reworking of the Imperial Japanese Army's current heavy machine gun, the Type 3, in the larger calibre. For reasons that remain unexplained, the opportunity was not taken in the development of the Type 92 to remove two of the Type 3's main disadvantages, namely the oil lubrication mechanism for the cartridges before they entered the gun, and the Hotchkiss type of strip feed.

The Type 92 became the Japanese Army's standard heavy machine gun and remained in service throughout World War II, in which it was supplemented by the Heavy Machine Gun Type 1, a lightened version with a shorter barrel. This weapon was robust and reliable overall, and served throughout Word War II, giving frontline troops sound machine-gun support.

LMG TYPE 99

The Light Machine Gun Type 99 was the best Japanese machine gun used in World War II after being introduced in 1939. The Type 99 weapon was developed from the 6.5mm Type 96, in a fashion analogous to the evolution of the Type 92 heavy machine gun from the Type 3 weapon, to use the new and somewhat higher-powered 7.7mm round in its definitive Type 99 rimless form. The Type 99 was a more fully optimized weapon than the Type 92, however, and the use of the rimless round meant that the system for oil lubrication of fresh rounds could be omitted. The standard bipod arrangement towards the front of the barrel was retained, and supplemented in the new weapon by an adjustable monopod under the butt's heel for greater stability when the gun was being fired at a long-range target. In other respects the Type 96 and Type 99 weapon were essentially identical, to the extent that even the entirely superfluous bayonet fitting was retained. There was also a Parachute Type Machine Gun Type 92 for the use of airborne forces: this could be broken down into three parts for ease of movement. Unfortunately for the men of the Imperial Japanese Army, production of the Type 99 machine gun never reached the figure that would have allowed the replacement of all its older light machine guns.

SPECIFICATIONS

LMG TYPE 99

Type:
light air-cooled machine gun

Calibre:
7.7mm (0.303in)

Length:
1.19m (46.75in)

Length of barrel:
0.545m (21.5in)

Weight:
10.4kg (23lb)

Muzzle velocity:
715m (2346ft) per second

Feed:
30-round detachable box magazine (850rpm)

GEVAER M/1894

SPECIFICATIONS

GEVAER M/1894

Type:
bolt-action rifle

Calibre:
6.5mm (0.256in)

Length:
1.27m (49.9in)

Length of barrel:
0.765mm (30.1in)

Weight:
4.05kg (8.9lb)

Muzzle velocity:
about 800m (2625ft) per second

Feed:
5-round detachable straight box magazine

The first service rifle based on the indigenous Krag-Jorgensen bolt action and righthand-side magazine to enter Norwegian service was the Gevaer m/1894 firing a Mauser 6.5mm rimless cartridge. Production of this weapon was initially undertaken both in Austria-Hungary (by Steyr) and in Norway (by the Kongsberg arsenal), but the majority of the rifles were made in Norway. The m/1894 was without doubt a capable and reliable weapon that was excellently made of high-quality materials, and was still the Norwegian Army's standard rifle at the time Germany overran Norway between April and June 1940.

The Germans then seized the surviving weapons for service with the revised designation 6.5mm Gewehr 211(n). The rifle was also produced in sniper and carbine versions. For sniping there were the Skarpskyttergevaer m/1923 with a telescopic sight to the left of the bolt action, the Skarpskyttergevaer m/1925 differing only in the stock, and the Skarpskyttergevaer m/1930 which had the look of a sporting weapon as it lacked a forestock and had no provision for a bayonet.

The carbine variants were the m/1895, m/1897, m/1904, m/1907 and m/1912 that differed from each other mainly in their stocks and swivels. Overall this weapon was a robust one.

PISTOL M1911

The M1911 semi-automatic was first produced in 1911 by Colt to one of the classic designs by John M. Browning, who created the weapon as a short-range pistol capable of halting and throwing back a charging man. After that the pistol became one of the most important military sidearms ever produced.

The baseline M1911 was widely used in World War I, and an assessment of the weapon's performance in that conflict resulted, during 1926, in the introduction of the M1911A1 definitive model (specifications for this model are given in the table at right). This differed from its predecessor mainly in the shaping of the grip with finger cuts behind the trigger, the lengthening and smoothing of the trigger, the size of the grip safety, and the alteration of the rifling.

In World War II the M1911A1 was used by many Allied forces in addition to those of the USA, one of these other users being the UK where some of the weapons were revised to 11.56mm (0.455in) calibre. The pistol was also made under licence in countries such as Spain and Norway (11.25mm automatisk pistol modell 1914, later used by the Germans as the Pistole 657[n]). Other pistols used by the Germans received the generic designation P 660(a). This pistol is still in service in parts of the world.

SPECIFICATIONS

PISTOL M1911

Type:
semi-automatic pistol

Calibre:
11.43mm (0.45in)

Length:
0.218m (8.6in)

Length of barrel:
0.128m (5.03in)

Weight:
1.1kg (2.44lb)

Muzzle velocity:
262m (860ft) per second

Feed:
7-round detachable straight box magazine

SPRINGFIELD M1903

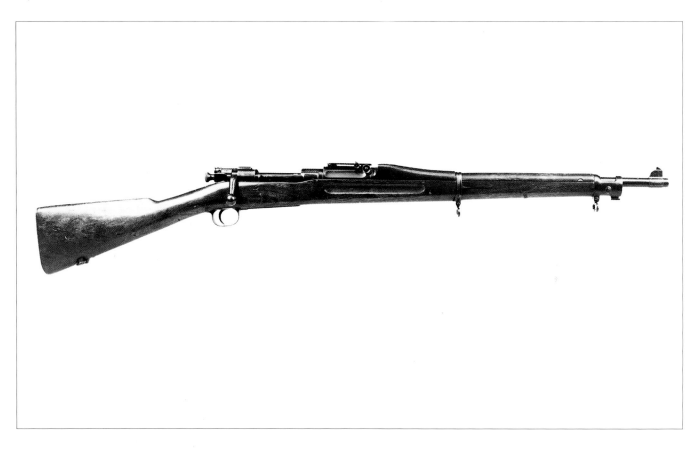

SPECIFICATIONS

SPRINGFIELD M1903

Type:
   bolt-action rifle

Calibre:
   7.62mm (0.3in)

Length:
   1.105m (43.5in)

Length of barrel:
   0.61m (24in)

Weight:
   4.1kg (9lb)

Muzzle velocity:
   855m (2805ft) per second

Feed:
   5-round fixed box magazine

It was in 1903 that the US Army standardized as its infantry rifle a modified version of the short Mauser rifle, and this was generally known as the "Springfield" for the arsenal in which it was first manufactured. The Model 1903 had the look of a typical Mauser rifle but, being of the short type, could also be used by cavalry and second-line units. The M1903 was the USA's standard rifle in World War I and the period following it, but although the M1 semi-automatic rifle was standardized as its successor in the 1930s, the bolt-action rifle remained in large-scale service right up to the end of World War II in 1945. During the USA's involvement in World War II from December 1941 there were three primary variants of the M1903 in service. The M1903A1 was adopted in 1939 and had a pistol-grip stock and a serrated trigger. The M1903A3 was introduced in May 1942 with features such as stamped steel components and simplified sights to facilitate production. The M1903A4 was introduced in December 1942 as the sniper counterpart of the M1903A3 with a x2.5 telescopic sight and no iron sights. The M1903 rifle was delivered in large numbers to American allies, especially China, and numbers were also handed over to guerrilla forces in Burma and the Philippines. The Germans allocated small numbers of captured weapons, known by the designation 7.62mm Gewehr 239(a).

M1 RIFLE

The Rifle M1 was the first semi-automatic rifle to enter full service anywhere in the world, being standardized for US service in 1932. Despite a major production programme that saw the delivery by 1945 of more than 5.5 million such rifles, however, the weapon did not entirely supersede the M1903 in World War II. The M1 rifle was known to virtually every soldier as the "Garand" after its creator, John C. Garand.

The M1 rifle was a well-designed weapon that was always well manufactured in a process that was somewhat expensive but yielded a weapon that was effective and reliable. There was a large number of experimental models, but the other two production variants in addition to the standard rifle were the M1C and M1D sniper versions standardized in June and September 1944, respectively.

A gas-operated weapon, the M1 rifle was fed with ammunition from an eight-round magazine that retained the charger clip until the last round was fired: this meant that the magazine could not be topped up with single rounds, and that the distinctive sound of the clip's ejection signalled both the firer's position and the fact that his weapon was empty. The German Army used captured M1 rifles with the designation 7.62mm Selbstladegewehr 251(a).

SPECIFICATIONS

M1 RIFLE

Type:
semi-automatic rifle

Calibre:
7.62mm (0.3in)

Length:
1.107m (43.6in)

Length of barrel:
0.609m (24in)

Weight:
4.31kg (9.5lb)

Muzzle velocity:
855m (2805ft) per second

Feed:
8-round fixed magazine

M1 CARBINE

SPECIFICATIONS

M1 CARBINE

Type:
 semi-automatic carbine

Calibre:
 7.63mm (0.3in)

Length:
 0.904m (35.6in)

Length of barrel:
 0.457m (18in)

Weight:
 2.36kg (5.2lb)

Muzzle velocity:
 600m (1970ft) per second

Feed:
 15- or 30-round detachable straight box magazine

In 1940 the US Army decided to adopt an automatic carbine to replace the pistol that had been the personal weapon of combat troops other than the infantry up to that time. Late in the same year there were trials of a number of contending weapons, of which a Winchester semi-automatic carbine emerged as the winner. This was standardized as the Carbine M1 (specifications for this weapon are given in the table at left), which had a unique gas-operated mechanism and in service revealed itself to be a very successful and popular weapon.

The M1 carbine was soon issued to frontline troops as well as its originally conceived recipients, and as a result production of this trim weapon exceeded 6.3 million units in Word War II – a figure greater than that of any other American weapon of the period. The one failing of the M1 carbine was its special cartridge, which lacked adequate power and therefore limited the carbine to short- and medium-range use.

The M1 carbine's sole major variant was the M1A1 with a folding stock for service with airborne troops. German special forces units used small numbers of captured carbines with the designation 7.63mm Selbstladekarabiner 455(a). The M1 carbine was one of the great weapons of World War II.

THOMPSON M1928

Designed in World War I, the submachine gun designed by J.T. Thompson did not enter production with the Auto-Ordnance Corporation until 1921. The Model 1921 was produced in some numbers as a retarded-blowback weapon chambered for the standard 11.43mm (0.45in) pistol cartridge carried in several types of magazine including a not very successful 100-round drum magazine but more commonly 50-round drum and 20-round vertical box magazines. The drum magazine model entered folklore as the weapon of American gangsters, a myth largely started and perpetuated by Hollywood.

The Model 1928 was a modest improvement with features such as the Cutts compensator (specifications for this weapon are given in the table at right) to help control muzzle climb. The US Navy bought small numbers, but in 1939 the British and French armies ordered large numbers. From June 1940 the French weapons were taken over by the Germans with the designation Maschinenpistole 760(f), and other such weapons entered the German inventory via the Baltic states, the USSR and Yugoslavia, whose weapons became MP 760(j) submachine guns. In the USA the Model 1928 was issued to cavalry units as the M1928A1. Overall this weapon was a very sound design.

SPECIFICATIONS

THOMPSON M1928

Type:
submachine gun

Calibre:
11.43mm (0.45in)

Length:
0.857m (33.75in)

Length of barrel:
0.267mm (10.52in)

Weight:
4.88kg (10.75lb)

Muzzle velocity:
280m (920ft) per second

Feed:
20- or 30-round box, or 50-round drum (600–725rpm)

SMG M1

SPECIFICATIONS

SMG M1

Type:
submachine gun

Calibre:
11.43mm (0.45in)

Length:
0.813m (32in)

Length of barrel:
0.267m (10.52in)

Weight:
4.74kg (10.45lb)

Muzzle velocity:
280m (920ft) per second

Feed:
20- or 30-round detachable box magazine (700rpm)

During the 1930s efforts were made to reduce the complexity, and thus the cost and manufacturing time, of the Model 1928. The weapon was therefore adapted with a more simple blowback operating system and the omission of features such as the compensator, the barrel cooling fins and the removable butt stock. European expedience had revealed the 50-round drum magazine to be noisy and too bulky, especially for use on the battlefield, so provision was made only for the two sizes of straight magazine. This resulted in the Gun, Sub-machine, Caliber .45, M1, of which more than one million had been completed before the end of World War II in 1945.

The M1A1 variant was the result of further simplification in which the original separate firing pin and hammer were replaced by a fixed firing pin. The M1 and M1Al were often preferred by troops to later weapons such as the M3, and the types were delivered in large numbers to the forces of other Allied powers. The types were especially popular in the Far East, and the Chinese produced their own version to succeed their clone of the M1928A1. Its popularity stemmed from the fact that it was a very robust and reliable weapon, and could be easily maintained in the field – an absolute necessity for Chinese forces.

SMG M3

In 1942 the US Army trialled several types of sub-machine guns, but none of these fully met the service's requirement. The staff at the Aberdeen Proving Grounds then created a simple design as the T15, which was thoroughly tested and paved the way to the improved T20 that was standardized for service as the Gun, Sub-machine, Caliber .45, M3.

The M3 was modelled closely on the Sten gun, which had been evaluated in the USA, but introduced changes such as ammunition feed from a vertical 30-round box magazine based on that of a German weapon, the Maschinenpistole 40. Initial service reaction was lukewarm, but the M3 then became popular as it showed itself to be effective and reliable, being nicknamed the "Grease Gun".

Mass production requirements had been designed into the weapon, which made extensive use of stamped and forged components in place of machine items, and this meant that general engineering companies were able to deliver more than 600,000 of the weapons by the end of the war in 1945. The M3A1 was a development that took the simplification of the design a stage further, replaced the breakable bolt retraction handle with a finger hole in the bolt, and increased the size of the ejection port.

SPECIFICATIONS

SMG M3

Type:
submachine gun

Calibre:
11.43 mm (0.45in)

Length:
0.757m (29in) extended; 0.579m (22.8in) retracted

Length of barrel:
0.203m (8in)

Weight:
3.7kg (8.15lb)

Muzzle velocity:
about 280m (920ft) per second

Feed:
30-round detachable box magazine (350–450rpm)

BAR

SPECIFICATIONS

BAR

Type:
light machine gun

Calibre:
7.62mm (0.3in)

Length:
1.214m (47.8in)

Length of Barrel :
0.611m (24.07in)

Weight:
8.73kg (19.4lb)

Muzzle velocity:
808m (2650ft) per second

Feed:
20-round detachable box magazine (300–350rpm)

While to the US forces the classic Browning Automatic Rifle, or BAR, was just that, to others the weapon was a light machine gun. The BAR was introduced to provide the US infantry involved in World War I with a weapon to bolster their firepower, and in World War II was the standard squad support weapon. The three primary models of this elegant weapon were the original Model 1918 hand-operated gun with no bipod but with a simple tube-type flash hider, the Model 1918A1 with a bipod and shoulder strap, and the Model 1918A2 (specification at left) with a butt monopod and the bipod (with plate rather than spiked feet) moved forwards from the front of the gas cylinder to the flash hider. The M1918A2 had two rates of automatic fire rather than the earlier models' selective fire capability, but this feature was sometimes removed. In Belgium the FN company also produced the BAR as its Fusil Mitrailleur modèle 1930 based on the M1918A1 and exported in 7, 7.65 and 7.92mm calibres. Captured Belgian weapons were used by the Germans with the designation 7.65mm le MG 727(b), while the 7.92mm Reczny karabin maszynowy wz.28 weapons seized in Poland became 7.9mm le MG 154(p) guns. Polish weapons seized by the USSR became 7.92mm Rutschnoi pulemet Browning obrazets 1928 guns.

M1917

Unlike other Browning automatic weapons of its period, the machine gun that entered service as the Machine Gun, Caliber .30in, M1917 was designed from the late 1890s with recoil rather than gas operation, and this was so successful that all subsequent Browning automatic weapons used the same system.

The M1917 looked similar to the Vickers gun except for its single pistol grip rather than twin spade grips, and large-scale production followed. The M1917, of which more than 68,000 were completed, was succeeded in 1936 by the M1917A1 (specifications for this particular model are given in the table at right) of which more than 54,000 were produced with changes in the sight, feed and tripod mounting, and this was the standard support machine gun operated by the US Army during World War II.

The Polish Ciezki karabin maszynowy wz.30 version found its way into German and Soviet hands after the country's conquest and partition in 1939, Germany calling the type the 7.9mm s MG 249(p) and the Soviets shortening the Polish designation to CKM wz.30. Up to 1939 the FN company in Belgium produced the weapon under licence for export, mainly to South American nations. The M1917 was a fine weapon, and gave good service to its users.

SPECIFICATIONS

M1917

Type:
medium water-cooled machine gun

Calibre:
7.62mm (0.3in)

Length:
0.981m (38.64in)

Length of barrel:
0.607m (23.9in)

Weight:
14.7kg (32.6lb) without cooling water

Muzzle velocity:
854m (2800ft) per second

Feed:
250-round fabric or metal link belt (450–600rpm)

M1919

SPECIFICATIONS

M1919

Type:
light air-cooled machine gun

Calibre:
7.62mm (0.3in)

Length:
1.041m (41in)

Length of barrel:
0.61m (24in)

Weight:
13.95kg (31lb)

Muzzle velocity:
854m (2800ft) per second

Feed:
250-round fabric or metal link belt (400–500rpm)

The Machine Gun, Caliber .30in, M1919 was basically an air-cooled development of the M1917 water-cooled machine gun, and was originally designed for use in tanks that were not produced. The M1917 was therefore developed as the M1919A1 for the infantry, the M1919A2 for the cavalry and the M1919A3, but none of these was made in large numbers and there followed the M1919A4 (specification at left) for service either in armoured vehicles or on a tripod mounting.

This was one of the definitive machine guns of World War II, in whose course almost 440,000 were manufactured for service with most Allied nations. The M1919A5 was a development of the M1919A4 specifically for use in armoured vehicles, and finally there arrived the M1919A6 infantry squad weapon that was the M1919A4 with a bipod, butt and carrying handle. A weapon of which almost 43,500 examples were manufactured, the M1919A6 was as successful in service as the M1919A4, and like this weapon became very popular despite the fact that it was slightly on the heavy side by the standards of other light machine guns. It is worth noting that the M1919 was also the basis for the M2 series of medium machine guns that were the core of US warplanes' armament in the period before and into World War II.

M2

The first machine gun designed by John Browning in 12.7mm (0.5in) calibre was the Model 1921 that was based on a scaled-up version of the action of the 7.62mm (0.3in) M1917 gun to fire a 0.5in round derived from the 13mm (0.512in) round of the Germans' T-Gewehr anti-tank rifle. The Model 1921 and improved Model 1921A were subsequently developed into the Machine Gun, Caliber .50in, M2 that was itself the starting point for a family of heavy machine guns all using the same mechanism and differing only in their types of barrel and installation. One of the first variants was the M2, which was a water-cooled weapon used in the anti-aircraft role (examples of this variant are shown in the photograph) and installed on many of the US Navy's ships. Another variant was the M2HB (heavy barrel) air-cooled weapon (specification at right) intended mainly for use in fixed installations, armoured vehicles and aircraft. There was also a downgraded variant of the M2 which had a lighter barrel and was therefore not usable for the sustained-fire role.

The M2 series was manufactured in very large numbers (greater than that of any other American machine gun), and in 1944 a development of the M2 with a higher rate of fire was introduced as the M3 for aircraft installations.

SPECIFICATIONS

M2

Type:
heavy air-cooled machine gun

Calibre:
12.7mm (0.5in)

Length:
1.65m (65.1in)

Length of barrel:
1.14m (45in)

Weight:
38.1kg (84lb) gun; 19.95kg (44lb) tripod mounting

Muzzle velocity:
866m (2840ft) per second

Feed:
110-round metal link belt (450–550rpm)

NAGANT 1895

SPECIFICATIONS

NAGANT 1895

Type:
revolver pistol

Calibre:
7.62mm (0.3in)

Length:
0.23m (9.055in)

Length of barrel:
0.11m (4.35in)

Weight:
0.795kg (1.75lb)

Muzzle velocity:
272m (892ft) per second

Feed:
7-round cylinder

The Belgian-designed Nagant revolver of 1895 was the standard Russian Army pistol in both world wars, but initially entered production in Liège before a Russian production facility was launched in Tula after the weapon's adoption for Russian service.

The Nagant revolver had several unusual features including the efforts made to create a gas-tight seal between the revolving cylinder and the barrel: the special round fired by the revolver had the tip of the bullet flush with the front of the cartridge, and the cylinder was also shifted forward against the rear of the barrel as the hammer was cocked.

There were single- and double-action variants of the revolver, these being issued to enlisted men and officers respectively. In overall terms the revolver was sturdy in its design and construction, the Germans using captured examples with the designation Revolver 612(r) to complement the R 612(p) weapons taken from the Poles in 1939. Greece also used the Nagant revolver in two forms, the Model 1895 being complemented by the Model 1912. Overall, though the design was sound, the weapon was an unremarkable piece, although for service on the Eastern Front, which was subject to wide temperature extremes and terrain variations, it performed well enough.

TULA-TOKAREVA 30-33

The two versions of the Soviets' Pistolet Tula-Tokareva (pistol made at Tula and designed by Fedor V. Tokarev), namely the obrazets 1930 and obrazets 1933, were better known as the TT30 and TT33 respectively. Both were based on the well-established Browning pistol design, from which they differed mainly in the use of a "packaged" sear and hammer assembly installed and removed as a unit, and the TT33 differed from the TT30 baseline model mainly in features designed to facilitate and therefore cheapen and speed production.

The TT33 was manufactured in altogether larger numbers than the TT30 in a programme that lasted until well after the end of World War II, and despite the decline in production standards as this war took its toll on the USSR's industrial capabilities, the TT33 remained an effective sidearm that was sturdy and reliable.

In the period of their great advances into the USSR during the second half of 1941, the Germans seized sufficient examples of the TT30 and TT33 to undertake a relatively wide distribution of what was now the Pistole 615(r) to the army and army force. As with most Red Army small arms, the Tula was easy to strip and re-assemble in the field, which meant maintenance was relatively easy and straightforward. However, as mentioned above, parts quality was variable.

SPECIFICATIONS

TULA-TOKAREVA 30-33

Type:
semi-automatic pistol

Calibre:
7.62mm (0.3in)

Length:
0.195m (7.68in)

Length of barrel:
0.116m (4.57in)

Weight:
0.854kg (1.88lb)

Muzzle velocity:
420m (1378ft) per second

Feed:
8-round detachable straight box magazine

MOSIN-NAGANT M1891

SPECIFICATIONS

MOSIN-NAGANT M1891

Type:
bolt-action rifle

Calibre:
7.62mm (0.3in)

Length:
1.305m (51.37in)

Length of barrel:
0.802m (31.2in)

Weight:
4.37kg (9.62lb)

Muzzle velocity:
810m (2660ft) per second

Feed:
5-round fixed box magazine

It was in 1891 that the Imperial Russian Army standardized the Mosin-Nagant rifle that combined features created by the Belgian Nagin brothers (magazine) and the Russian Colonel N.I. Mosin (action). The Russkaya 3-linenaye vintovka obrazets 1891 was developed when a standard Russian unit of distance was the "line", almost exactly 2.54mm, so the three "lines" of the calibre were thus 7.62mm. The obrazets 1891 (see specification) was the standard Russian rifle of World War I in a form with updated sights and improved ammunition, and remained in service after the Soviet revolution right through to the USSR's involvement in World War II. Although the Germans captured large numbers of these rifles in 1941, the calibration of their sights in non-metric units meant that only a limited distribution was made of what was now known as the 7.62mm Gewehr 252(r). A variant for cavalry use was also produced from 1891 with a shortened barrel. Other countries who used the rifle were Yugoslavia (Puska 7.62mm M91R bought from the USSR), Poland (karabin wz.91/98/25 produced locally with a shorter barrel and some Mauser-type furniture and fittings) and Finland (Russian actions combined with otherwise indigenous manufacture to create the m/27 shorter than the obrazets 1891, and m/28, the m/28/30).

MOSIN-NAGANT M91/30

The vintovka obrazets 1891/30 was a shortened development of the obrazets 1891 rifle with more modern sights and changes to facilitate mass production. The obrazets 1891/30 was the Soviet Army's standard rifle through the "Great Patriotic War" with Germany between 1941 and 1945, and was also produced in a sniper model that could be fitted with either the PU x3.5 or PE x4 telescopic sight, and had a turned-down bolt handle to avoid hitting the telescopic sight.

These weapons entered service in 1937, and became a major component in the Soviets' World War II propaganda extolling the courage and skill of snipers. Oddly enough for a service rifle, the obrazets 1891/30 could also be fitted with a silencer, but a more natural adjunct was the Granatomet Djakonowa obrazets 1930, which was a cup-type grenade launcher for attachment to the muzzle; this was used in conjunction with a special sight and a bipod attached under the forestock.

The Germans captured very large numbers of obrazets 1891/30 rifles in 1941 and 1942, and these were issued with the revised designation 7.62mm Gewehr 254(r) to German second-line forces as well as anti-Soviet units raised from prisoners of war.

SPECIFICATIONS

MOSIN-NAGANT M1891/30

Type:
bolt-action rifle

Calibre:
7.62mm (0.3in)

Length:
1.232m (48.5in)

Length of barrel:
0.729m (28.7in)

Weight:
4kg (8.8lb)

Muzzle velocity:
810m (2657ft) per second

Feed:
5-round fixed box magazine

MOSIN-NAGANT M1938

SPECIFICATIONS

MOSIN-NAGANT M1938

Type:
bolt-action carbine

Calibre:
7.62mm (0.3in)

Length:
1.016m (40in)

Length of barrel:
0.508m (20in)

Weight:
3.47kg (7.6lb)

Muzzle velocity:
765m (2510ft) per second

Feed:
5-round fixed box magazine

As was inevitable at a time when horsed cavalry was considered as important as, if not actually more significant than, the infantry, the Russians needed a shorter version of its long infantry rifle that could be carried in a cavalryman's saddle holster and also serve as the personal weapon of troops such as gunners. The first genuine carbine version of the Mosin-Nagant rifle was the karabin obrazets 1910. Only limited production was undertaken of this weapon, which was in essence a truncated version of the obrazets 1891 rifle and could not be fitted with a bayonet.

Cavalry continued to be important to the Soviets in the period before World War II, and this led to the development of the karabin obrazets 1938 (see specification), which was basically the karabin obrazets 1910 upgraded to vintovka 1891/30 standard, and the Germans used captured examples with the designation Karabiner 453(r).

The final version was the karabin obrazets 1944, which was in fact the last Mosin-Nagant weapon to enter production. This differed from the obrazets 1938 weapon only in its permanently attached folding bayonet. The German Army used limited numbers of captured weapons on the Eastern Front with the designation Karabiner 457(r).

SIMONOV 1936

The first semi-automatic rifle placed in service by the Soviet Army, the Avtomaticheskaya vintovka Simonova obrazets 1936 (AVS or AVS36) was designed from the early 1930s by S.G. Simonov. Despite a lengthy period of intensive development, however, this gas-operated self-loading weapon was not successful. Perhaps to ensure that the weapon, which was comparatively expensive to produce, would offer capability in more than one role, it was fitted with a selector that permitted the firer to deliver single-shot or automatic fire. This latter suggests that a light machine gun capability in the rifle section support role was envisaged, but the high level of muzzle blast and flash made this impossible and also required the installation of combined compensator and muzzle brake that was efficient in neither task. Another difficulty was that the design of the action meant that the bolt handle travelled to and fro in an open slot: this was dangerous to the firer and also allowed dirt to enter and jam the operating mechanism. The AVS was accordingly pulled out of service from 1938, although there were still examples in service (mainly with second-line forces and, in a form with a telescopic sight, snipers) at the time of Germany's 1941 invasion. The Germans used small numbers with the designation Selbstladegewehr 257(r).

SPECIFICATIONS

SIMONOV 1936

Type:
semi-automatic rifle

Calibre:
7.62mm (0.3in)

Length:
12.34m (48.6in)

Length of barrel:
0.614m (24.16in)

Weight:
4.05kg (8.93lb) without the magazine

Muzzle velocity:
840m (2756ft) per second

Feed:
15-round detachable straight box magazine

TOKAREV M1940

SPECIFICATIONS

TOKAREV M1940

Type:
semi-automatic rifle

Calibre:
7.62mm (0.3in)

Length:
1.222m (48.1in)

Length of barrel:
0.625m (24.6in)

Weight:
3.89kg (8.56lb)

Muzzle velocity:
830m (2723ft) per second

Feed:
10-round detachable straight box magazine

Realizing that the operating system of the SVT38 was too flimsy for service use but technically sound, the Soviet authorities ordered further development to create the Samozariadniya vintovka Tokareva obrazets 1940 (SVT40) (specifications for this weapon are given in the table at left). This was a beefed-up weapon that possessed adequate strength, but was still unpopular with the troops in the field for its strong recoil. Examples selected for their accuracy were revised to carry a telescopic sight for use in the sniping role.

Two other variants were a shortened carbine model, of which small numbers were produced either as conversions of existing rifles or as new-production weapons, and a selective-fire model capable of being used in the rifle section support role. This latter was the Avtomaticheskaya vintovka Tokareva obrazets 1940 (AVT40) with a selector allowing fully automatic fire. Again only modest numbers were made, but the Germans were impressed with the type, copying the Tokarev action for use in their own Gewehr 43, and using captured SVT40 weapons with the designation Selbstladegewehr 259(r) and, in the case of those fitted with a telescopic sight, Sl Gew Zf260(r). The Tokarev was, like most Soviet weapons, a sturdy design that could withstand a lot of punishment.

PPD34/38

Designed by Vasili A. Degtyarev for service from 1934, the Pistolet-Pulemet Degtyareva obrazets 1934 and improved PPD obrazets 1934/38 submachine guns derived some of their features from a pair of foreign weapons, the Finnish m/1931 and the German MP 28/II. The first model drew its ammunition from a 73-round drum magazine but the second model used a 71-round drum magazine copied from that of the Finnish weapon. The final model, based on the second, had a simplified barrel jacket characterized by three sets of larger slots in place of the earlier models' eight sets of smaller slots.

It is believed that it was 1940 when production of this pioneering Soviet weapon ended at the two factories tasked with its manufacture. The weapon was conventional in its blowback operation, and the only notable feature of its construction was the chromed interior of the barrel (to reduce wear and thus extend life), which became standard on Soviet submachine guns. In 1941 and 1942 the Germans captured large numbers of PPD submachine guns, which they placed in service with the designation Maschinenpistole 716(r) firing either captured Soviet ammunition or the Mauser 7.63mm pistol round that was dimensionally identical to the Soviet type.

SPECIFICATIONS

PPD34/38

Type:
submachine gun

Calibre:
7.62mm (0.3in)

Length:
0.777m (30.6in)

Length of barrel:
0.273m (10.75in)

Weight:
3.74kg (8.25lb)

Muzzle velocity:
490m (1608ft) per second

Feed:
71-round drum or 25-round box magazine (800rpm)

PPD38/40

SPECIFICATIONS

PPD38/40

Type:
submachine gun

Calibre:
7.62mm (0.3in)

Length:
0.787m (31in)

Length of barrel:
0.26m (10.5in)

Weight:
3.63kg (8lb)

Muzzle velocity:
490m (1608ft) per second

Feed:
71-round detachable drum magazine (800rpm)

The Pistolet-Pulemet Degtyareva obrazets 1940 (PPD40) was a development of the original PPD designed to facilitate production, and was introduced in time for service in the later stages of the Russo-Finnish "Winter War" of 1939–40.

Despite the fact that it had been re-designed to speed production and, wherever possible, reduce manufacturing costs, the PPD38/40 was still produced from high-quality materials in the fashion typical of peace- rather than wartime planning, and as a result was taken out of production in 1941 after the German invasion of the Soviet Union.

Although the PPD38/40 resembled its predecessor in many respects, and indeed benefited from the interchangeability of many of its components, it had a different bolt and drew its ammunition from a new type of 71-round drum magazine: this latter fitted into a recess in the underside of the receiver rather than having a tongue that was pushed up into a hole in the receiver as in the earlier weapon. The weapon was effective and reliable, and as a result the Germans used all such weapons that they captured with the revised designation Maschinenpistole 715(r). Both sides continued to use this weapon on the Eastern Front until the end of the war.

PPSH41

The German invasion in the second half of 1941 cost the USSR not only vast amounts of territory, people and matériel, but also much of the country's industrial capability. The urgent need for rearmament had to be undertaken in this context, and one of the answers was a submachine gun that could be produced quickly and cheaply. This weapon emerged as the Pistolet-Pulemet Shpagina obrazets 1941 (PPSh41) designed by Georgi S. Shpagin. The weapon entered service in 1942, and was so easy to manufacture that more than five million had been delivered by the end of World War II in 1945.

The PPSh41 was simple in concept and basic design, which meant that production could be undertaken with only the most limited requirement for machining. While its finish was generally poor, with the exception of the chromed interior of the barrel, the weapon was effective and thoroughly reliable under the many types of difficult operating conditions typical of the titanic war on the Eastern Front.

Complete battalions were sometimes equipped with the PPSh41, and the weapon so impressed the Germans that they used captured weapons, revised to 9mm Parabellum calibre and a housing to accept the magazine of the MP 40, with the designation 9mm Maschinenpistole 717(r).

SPECIFICATIONS

PPSH41

Type:
submachine gun

Calibre:
7.62mm (0.3in)

Length:
0.840m (33.1in)

Length of barrel:
0.269m (10.6in)

Weight:
3.5kg (7.7lb)

Muzzle velocity:
490m (1608ft) per second

Feed:
35-round box magazine or 71-drum (900–1000rpm)

PPS43

PPS43

Type:
submachine gun

Calibre:
7.62mm (0.3in)

Length:
0.907m (35.7in) extended; 0.641m (25.25in) folded

Length of barrel:
0.273m (10.75in)

Weight:
3.33kg (7.34lb)

Muzzle velocity:
490m (1608ft) per second

Feed:
35-round detachable box magazine (700rpm)

The submachine gun generally known as the PPS42 (Pistolet-Pulemet Sudareva obrazets 1942) was developed and first produced under the most adverse of conditions, namely the German siege of Leningrad, which lasted from the autumn of September 1941 until early 1944. To provide the forces holding the city with an effective close-range weapon that could be manufactured inside the defensive perimeter, A. I. Sudarev designed a submachine gun assembled almost completely from of spit-welded, pinned or riveted steel stampings with wood or plastic for the pistol grips only and a folding metal butt instead of the otherwise standard wooden butt.

So successful was the PPS42 (specifications given in the table at left) that the basic type was kept in production, after the lifting of Leningrad's siege, as the improved PPS43 that was nevertheless still more simple to manufacture than the PPS42: the metal stock was shortened, the safety mechanism and magazine housing were improved, and hard rubber pistol grips were introduced for ease of use.

More than one million PPS43 weapons were made, and the Germans used captured examples with the designation Maschinenpistole 709(r). Finland also produced an m/1944 in 9mm Parabellum calibre. This was one of the great weapons of the Eastern Front.

PM1910

Many types of machine gun have been based on the Maxim gun, but the heaviest and longest-lived of these is surely the Russian Pulemet Maksima obrazets 1905 (PM1905) and its successors. This was based on an entirely unchanged Maxim operating system, and had a bronze water-cooling jacket that was changed to steel in 1910 to create the PM1910.

Production of the PM1910 lasted to 1943 in a huge stream of weapons whose last examples were virtually indistinguishable from the first. The weapon was immensely strongly built and could take in its stride rough usage and all the adverse effects of terrain and weather. The few changes introduced over the gun's production life included a filler cap, derived from a tractor radiator cap, on top of the water jacket, but these were very minor add-ons.

The gun could be installed on many types of mounting, of which the most common was the Sokolov, in essence a small artillery carriage with a pair of steel wheels, a traversing turntable and a hand-towing trail. For the antiaircraft role the PM1910 was mounted on a special tripod. The PM1910 was used right through World War II, and the Germans operated captured examples with the designation schwere Maschinengewehr 216(r), generally in fixed defences.

SPECIFICATIONS

PM1910

Type:
heavy water-cooled machine gun

Calibre:
7.62mm (0.3in)

Length:
1.107m (43.6in)

Length of barrel:
0.72m (28.4in)

Weight:
23.8 kg (52.5 in) gun; 45.2kg (99.7lb) with shield

Muzzle velocity:
865m (2838ft) per second

Feed:
250-round fabric belt (520–600rpm)

DP

SPECIFICATIONS

DP

Type:
light air-cooled machine gun

Calibre:
7.62mm (0.3in)

Length:
1.265m (49.8in)

Length of barrel:
0.605m (23.8in)

Weight:
12.2kg (26.8lb)

Muzzle velocity:
845m (2772ft) per second

Feed:
47-round detachable drum magazine (520–580rpm)

The Pulemet Degtyareva Pekhotnii (DP) light machine gun was the first machine gun of wholly Russian design to enter service. Designed in the early 1920s by Vasili A. Degtyarev, the first model was trialled as the DP1926 in competition with two modified light Maxim guns and, with a certain number of modifications, was taken into service as the DP1928, generally shortened to DP, and immediately revealed itself to be a superb weapon characterized by light weight and a simple mechanism that was nonetheless strong and reliable. The gas-operated mechanism contained a mere six moving parts, and this helped to ensure that the DP remained serviceable under the most adverse geographic and climatic extremes.

The Soviets employed the DP in very large numbers right through their involvement in World War II, and the Germans used captured weapon with the designation 7.62mm leichte Maschinengewehr 120(r). The DP's only real failing was the tendency of the main spring to become hot during protracted firing and lose its strength, resulting in jams. This was remedied in the Pulemet Degtyareva Pekhotnii Modifikatsionii (DPM or DPM44) (see specification at left), which also had a pistol grip behind the trigger, a strengthened and improved bipod, and no grip safety.

DSHK38

It was in 1939 that the Krasnoi Pulemet Degtyereva-Shpagina obrazets 1938 (DShK38) entered Soviet service as a heavy machine gun in 12.7mm calibre based – unlike the tactically similar Browning M2 series with its recoil operation – on the Degtyarev type of gas-operated mechanism and a feed arrangement created by another celebrated Soviet small arms engineer, Georgi Shpagin.

The DShK38 was an extremely capable and successful weapon whose applications were gradually extended to include installation as the secondary armament of Soviet tanks, as well as on armoured trains and fast attack craft of various types. It was in the ground role that the DShK38 played its most important part in the Soviet victory over the Germans, though, and in this application the weapon was generally installed on the obrazets 1938 mounting adapted from that of another heavy machine gun, the 7.62mm PM1910. There was also a special anti-aircraft mounting to provide the gun with large angles of elevation and traverse. There were also twin and quadruple anti-aircraft mountings of the DShK38. This weapon was still being used by Russian and Afghan forces in Afghanistan during the Soviet occupation in the 1980s. It was an overall excellent and robust weapon.

SPECIFICATIONS

DSHK38

Type:
heavy air-cooled machine gun

Calibre:
12.7mm (0.5in)

Length:
1.602m (62.3in)

Length of barrel:
1.002m (39.4in)

Weight:
33.3kg (73.5lb)

Muzzle velocity:
845m (2772ft) per second

Feed:
250-round belt (550–600rpm)

INDEX